ROUGH JUSTICE

Crime and Punishment on the Northwest Frontier
& The Origins of Oregon State Penitentiary

Copyright © 2025 James O. Long

ROUGH JUSTICE:
CRIME AND PUNISHMENT ON THE NORTHWEST FRONTIER
& THE ORIGINS OF OREGON STATE PENITENTIARY

Copyright © 2025 by James O. Long

All rights reserved.

First paperback edition 2025
ISBN 978-1-735-12983-9

—U.S. History—State/local —Pacific Northwest/Oregon/Washington
—American exploration and expansion (1800-1861)
—Social Science—criminal justice law
Humor—history

This is a work of nonfiction, researched and written by a human being. All of the events really happened, and all of the characters were real people.

Edited and designed by Dee Lane & Jenny Niemeyer

No part of this publication may be reproduced, distributed, or transmitted in any form or by any means, including photocopying, recording, or other electronic or mechanical methods, without the prior written permission of the publisher, except in the case of brief quotations embodied in critical reviews and certain other noncommercial uses permitted by copyright law.

Published by Bottlefly Press, Boise ID
For permission requests write to the publisher: bottleflypress@gmail.com

Library of Congress Control Number 2025922883

10 9 8 7 6 5 4 3 2 1

Cover: "Great Register" listing some of the first inmates at the Oregon State Penitentiary and photo of early OSP prison guards. (Oregon Historical Society)

Author's Note

This book was decades in the making.

The beginning was a conversation I had with the late Thomas Vaughan, longtime executive director of the Oregon Historical Society. We were talking about the Oregon State Penitentiary, the state's maximum security prison, which was then one of my beats for The Oregonian newspaper. I spent a lot of time there as a reporter and dug into it the way I dug into anything I was assigned to cover.

Tom thought I was uniquely positioned to write about the penitentiary, and we agreed that a story going back to its origins would be fascinating.

That meant researching the days of the Oregon frontier and the Hudson's Bay Company. How did the first jail, or prison, come about? What was it like as it evolved?

We both thought that a story that just talked about wardens and guards and prison architecture would be dull. Not worth the time or trouble.

What would make it worthwhile was putting the prison in its setting. What was the Oregon frontier like when the Hudson's Bay Company ruled it? How did it change as the years passed? What sorts of crimes did the first settlers have to deal with, and how did they do it? What happened to lawbreakers when there were hardly any lawmen or judges and no regular place to keep prisoners if they were arrested? And how did this change over time?

Tom and I thought it would be an irresistible, crazy story full of vivid characters and outlandish situations. And it certainly was.

Time and circumstance and a demanding job at the newspaper did not allow this book to quick-march to completion, however. It had to wait. For years, parts of it sat on the shelf. I retired, took on other projects and thought about the book. Finally, I decided it was time to finish.

As we prepare to publish, the state prison that opened in the 1860s still exists. An "Oregon boot," the early shackle designed to keep prisoners from escaping, sits in a display near the superintendent's office. Just this year, the Department of Corrections suggested that it might be time to replace the prison.

As you'll see, some things never change.

"Show me your prisons and I'll tell you what kind of country you have."

—often attributed to
Winston Churchill

1.
An ornament of civilized society

Christmas night, when everyone at the Fort was having a good time, I hurd something hit the floor. At first I thought it was someone at the door. I began to feel around on the floor and I found what proved to be two brand-new files. Maybe you think I did not work fast! I think in about four hours I was entirely loose from le chaine. I waited for old Bruce, the jailer, who brought by breakfast. Six in the morning and it was quite dark yet. Presently I hurd him at the door. I made ready. I was on the side of the door, after he pushed the door in he got that pan that had the grub in and he layed on the floor and began to push as usual. I struck him on the side of the head, I pulled him in and I took his coat and cap, put them on, and started across the fort for the gate.

—Edouard "Frenchy" Chambreau,
Fort Vancouver, 1848[1]

The first jail in the Oregon Country—the one that held Frenchy Chambreau on Christmas 1848—was not the property of a government. It was built and operated by a private corporation, the Hudson's Bay Company.

The Honourable Company, as its officials called it, was chartered by the British Crown and granted extraordinary powers to conduct a fur-trade monopoly across much of North America. It thought of itself not so much as a private enterprise as an embodiment of Imperial Britain in the New World.

A Hudson's Bay official, standing at the gate of York Factory on Hudson Bay in northeast Manitoba, could look toward the setting sun and know with satisfaction that he could trek a greater distance than from London to Moscow without ever leaving the Company's dominion. At its zenith, the Empire of Hudson's Bay stretched across thousands of miles of forest and river from eastern Canada to the rugged shores of the North Pacific. "Oregon" was a vague term for that rich and varied expanse of the American continent west of the Rocky Mountains between Russian Alaska and Mexican California.

Hudson's Bay signaled its intent to put Oregon permanently in Britain's pocket by establishing a headquarters, Fort Vancouver, in a strategic location on the north shore of the Columbia River across from present-day Portland.

Named for British seaman and explorer George Vancouver, the fort's blunt log palisades were hammered and pegged together in years 1824-25, making a bold statement about the Company's authority and its place in the Empire. A red-slashed Union Jack fluttering above a gun tower reminded all, including any Americans who set foot in the territory, that the Hudson's Bay Company dealt not just in blankets and beaver pelts but in English law, and sovereignty.

Not surprisingly, the Chief Factor—superintendent—of a Company post as important as Fort Vancouver wielded considerable power. He was a civil governor with the peremptory authority of a military commander. His orders had the effect of law. And in many important ways, the Chief Factor was the law.

Company officials were responsible for keeping the peace and enforcing order wherever they operated. Above all they were responsible for the conduct of their own employees. Some Company officials got royal appointments as justices of the peace, with authority to arrest criminal suspects and dispose of them according to British law. They could hold courts of record and try any criminal case not involving the death penalty or transportation to a penal colony. They had jurisdiction in civil lawsuits involving disputes not exceeding 200 British Pounds. For more serious civil suits, three Company justices could sit as a fact-finding commission on behalf of a higher court in Canada. Or, if authorized, the justices could render judgment on the spot.[2]

Fort Vancouver's most noted chief factor, the one who built the fort and Oregon's first jail, was John McLoughlin, a former Montreal surgeon who had practiced for a year before laying aside his scalpel to enter the fur trade. One of the truly fascinating characters in American history, McLoughlin would not have seemed miscast in either the role of Old Testament prophet or sheriff of Dodge City. A man of dominating personality, with physique to match, McLoughlin stood well over six feet tall, was ruggedly built, transfixed visitors with blazing blue eyes, and had a mane of silvery hair—or so it became as the summers passed—reaching to his shoulders.

Sir George Simpson, the Company's North American viceroy, first shook hands with McLoughlin in August 1823. He wrote to a higher official that

> He [McLoughlin] was such a figure as I should not like to meet in a dark night in one of the byelanes of the neighborhood of London. He was dressed in Clothes that had once been fashionable but now covered with a thousand patches of different Colours, his beard would do honor to the chin of a Grizzly Bear, his face and hands evidently Shewing that he had not lost much time at his Toilette, loaded with arms and his own herculean dimensions forming a tout ensemble, that would convey a good idea of the highway-men of former days.

Simpson wasn't just trying to be amusing. He was a different sort of man than McLoughlin, ready to judge him and pass along the stories he heard about his cruelty. The stories weren't all rumor, but history would be kinder to McLoughlin than the scheming Simpson. Simpson's corporate flannel was a contrast to McLoughlin's basic humanity, flawed as it might be. Whatever else might be said about the chief factor of Fort Vancouver, it was hard to fault him for his generosity and courage.

Hundreds of American settlers who stumbled exhausted out of the wilderness after a harrowing trek to Oregon would all but owe their lives to McLoughlin. Despite Company instructions to the contrary—it didn't want to encourage American settlement—McLoughlin let many newcomers buy goods on credit, often with no more collateral than a handshake.

He dealt fairly with the Indians by the standards of his day, and, in a climate of strong religious bigotry, did his best to protect Fort Vancouver's Catholic minority.

Still, McLoughlin was an autocrat who could be merciless when crossed. He didn't mind having a man flogged, or worse, when his temper got the best of him, as it often did.

Within the savage context of 19th Century British criminal law, flogging was nothing out of the ordinary. It was the statutory punishment for any number of minor offenses such as vagrancy. And sometimes it was used to enhance a prison sentence if incarceration alone seemed too dainty. Hanging was not a neglected option although the number of crimes considered a capital offense had been reduced from 215 at the end of the 1600s to a mere 50 by the time Fort Vancouver was established.

Court records in 19th Century Britain show many instances of defendants sent to the gallows for offenses that would barely qualify as misdemeanors today. One man was hanged for stealing a handkerchief. A 14-year-old girl was hanged for stealing a silver spoon.

McLoughlin and his deputies didn't seem to draw much distinction between acts that were criminal and those they found obnoxious or inconvenient. Many a servant was flogged or put in irons, or both, for such things as "Insufficient attention to duty."

McLoughlin kept two or three old naval guns by his front porch where servants who vexed him were restrained and beaten. Different visitors described this artillery differently, with most referring to a pair of 18-pounders—guns sufficient to penetrate two feet of oak at 400 yards and sink a dreadnought. William H. Gray, a pioneer American clergyman and historian, said he saw a 24-pounder mounted on a ship's carriage and that it was flanked by two smaller mortar guns. The carriage, complete with stubby wheels, had been whitewashed nicely to match the rose trellises, Gray recalled.

McLoughlin's flogging equipment, whatever the details, sat in the curving embrace of two flights of stairs that ascended to the porch that commanded a view of the yard. The fort's officers tramped up and down the stairs several times daily for meals and also for business meetings held customarily in the Chief Factor's dining room, "the officer's mess." Visitors climbing the stairs could hardly have helped noticing the guns and may have assumed they were decorative. But the fort's residents knew better. They knew that anyone not of gentleman rank who ran afoul of McLoughlin was apt to be tied over a cannon barrel like a pig on a roasting-spit and given a public hiding.[4]

The most notorious flogging occurred in 1837 and involved a Company servant named William Brown. Brown's offense was refusing to re-enlist. The Rev. Herbert Beaver, the fort chaplain, said Brown was "stripped and tied up to one of the Great Guns, which stand at the foot of the mess room steps, the usual place and mode of administering corporal punishment, and ordered to receive two dozen lashes with a cat-o'-nine tails."[5] The sentence was carried out, Beaver said,

> by the messwaiter, a very powerful man, being, according to custom, the executioner, and a very severe left-handed flogger. On the sixth lash, which, by that reason and the awkwardness of the inflictor, fell across the heart, the poor man, whose courage now failed, said he was ready to go whither they pleased to send him, provided they would release him, which accordingly was done; Chief Factor McLoughlin and (James) Douglas, who superintended the punishment, no medical man, although one is stationed at the Fort, being present, telling him that they were sorry to inflict it upon a man, who bore an uniformly excellent character, but that orders must be obeyed.[6]

Later on, Brown made his way back to England where he complained at corporate headquarters. The Company's board of governors feared a messy lawsuit and asked McLoughlin to explain himself. McLoughlin replied that he whipped Brown not so much for trying to leave his job as for trying to leave Oregon without an infant son he had fathered. The mother was a Native woman Brown lived with in a "fur trade marriage." McLoughlin told the board that abandoned Native women sometimes killed such infants because neither they nor the child would be accepted back in the tribe.

Headquarters, however, was more concerned about liability in a lawsuit than the fate of babies and mothers. Even worse was the possibility of political blowback. Groups protesting the exploitation of indigenous peoples were becoming a political force and might cause the Company real trouble. On the advice of its lawyers, the board paid Brown £20 to keep quiet. It also sent McLoughlin a stiff letter informing him that "the corporal punishment inflicted was decidedly illegal. Had it gone to a court of law it might have subjected the Concern to disagreeable exposure."[7]

Physical coercion wasn't the only, or even most important, means of control available to McLoughlin. The Company hired its rank-and-file workers on five-year contracts at a salary of about £17 annually. The terms of the agreements required workers to obey orders, and wages could be withheld for breach of contract.[8] The Company enjoyed the advantage of deciding when a contract had been breached. However, it couldn't always fine an offending employee as often or as extravagantly as it wished because it didn't pay them enough.

Trappers Jean Marie Bouche and Louis Ossin, who were found guilty of desertion and stealing supplies at the Company's York Factory in Manitoba, had to be excused from financial punishment "owing to their embarrassed circumstances." Instead, they were "Hand cuffed and publicly exposed during one full day on the roof of the Factory," and afterwards imprisoned for a week on bread and water.[9]

There were other practical limits on the use of fines besides the inability of employees to pay. During Simpson's earlier days as the Company's North American viceroy, he complained bitterly to London that he couldn't punish his men as severely as he thought they deserved because he often had to bargain away penalties to get them to re-enlist.

> A common 'voyageur' does not hesitate to call his Master a 'Sacra Crap,' knowing that the offence must be overlooked when his contract expires," Simpson grumbled. "And when he is asked to renew his engagement, he not only insists on having all fines struck off his account but his Wages advanced about one-third and in some cases more.[10]

At Fort Vancouver, McLoughlin found an ingenious way to overcome the re-enlistment problem: He forced employees to eat their way into debt.

Lt. Charles Wilkes, an American naval officer who visited the fort in 1841, and who otherwise formed a good opinion of McLoughlin, couldn't help noticing that the workers' rations were miserable, apparently as a matter of policy. While McLoughlin and his officers ate well, enjoying wine with their dinner, the lower ranks picked through thin helpings of slop, Wilkes observed. He said the hungry men were thus encouraged to use their meager earnings to buy food at the Company store.

"When their time expires almost all are in debt," Wilkes wrote in his diary. "Consequently they are obliged to serve an extra time on the expiration of [their contract], & whilst they so continue they are as it were still bound to the Company and under their surveillance."[11]

Systematic fraud and abuse may have slowed the turnover rate at Vancouver but also made it harder to hire replacements. Things got so bad that Simpson resorted to filling vacancies with whatever specimens he could scrape up. When McLoughlin protested to London, Simpson said McLoughlin had brought it on himself. He said his reputation for severity was widespread and well-deserved and that few men who had a choice could be persuaded to go to Oregon.

The board sided gingerly with Simpson.

"We have learnt from other sources," the board of directors wrote McLoughlin, "that there is an insurmountable reluctance on the part of respectable laborers to accept employment on the west side of the Mountains, occasioned by the reports circulated by those who have returned from that quarter."

The board gave no details about the sorts of tales that were making the rounds, except to express confidence that these were exaggerated, surely. Nevertheless, the board took the opportunity to review with McLoughlin the Company policy on beating sense into employees. The board wrote:

> When bad men are associated together, or mixed with the good it will be impossible to preserve necessary discipline without having recourse sometimes to corporal punishment. But such punishment should never be inflicted under the influence of passion or caprice. To produce any good [a]ffect it should be administered with coolness

[of] temper and moderation, and at the same time with as much solemnity as circumstances will admit.[12]

To encourage McLoughlin to keep their advice in mind, the directors told him to report future floggings in writing.

Despite the indirection and the hemming and hawing, McLoughlin got the message which was "put the bloody brakes on the flogging." It wasn't that the board had suddenly grown a social conscience but that it was feeling political heat and feared the possible consequences. The reports coming out of Oregon had spiced up the London newspapers read by members of Parliament as well as Queen Victoria and the Prime Minister. All had to answer directly or indirectly to a public roused by a reform-minded clergy and growing army of do-gooders.

1. NOTES

1. *Autobiographical Narrative for Years 1847-80,* Edouard "Frenchy" Chambreau. Reed College Library collection. Portland OR.

2. George IV chapter 66, "An Act for regulating the Fur Trade and establishing a Criminal and Civil Jurisdiction within certain parts of North America," enacted by British parliament in 1821.

3. Simpson letter to Andrew Wedderburn, Lord Colville, the Company's deputy governor in London Aug. 9, 1824. Cited by E.E. Rich, ed., The Letters of John McLoughlin, 1st series 1825-38. The Champlain Society for the Hudson's Bay Record Society, London 1941, p. xxiv.

4. John McLoughlin's business letters made it clear he considered floggings indispensable for maintaining discipline. William H. Gray, a pioneer Oregon clergyman and judge, said Company employees "by the articles of enlistment, were bound to obey all orders of a superior officer, as much so as a soldier in the army. Flogging was a common punishment inflicted by all grades of officers, from a petty clerk of a trading post up to the governor of the company." See Gray's *A History of Oregon* (Portland: Harris & Holman, 1870), p 196. Gray and other writers gave slightly different accounts of the "whipping post" site in front of McLoughlin's house. Gray, who visited Fort Vancouver in April 1836, remembered a 24-pound ship's cannon sitting between two smaller mortar-guns. (op. cit., p. 150). John Wyeth, an American businessman who arrived in 1832, also mentioned seeing several 24-pound guns, but most other visitors mentioned 18-pounders. John Kirk Townsend, a natural scientist who dropped by in 1834, noted two "long 18's." The Rev. Herbert Beaver, the fort chaplain who arrived the same time as Gray, mentioned in his own writings that whippings took place customarily at one of the "big guns" in front of the "mess," or officers' dining room. See Herbert Beaver, *Reports and Letters of Herbert Beaver, 1836-38,* ed. Thomas E. Jessett. Champoeg Press, Portland OR 1959, p. 36.

5. Jessett, p. 36.

6. Beaver letter to Benjamin Harrison, governor of the Hudson's Bay Company in London. *Reports and Letters of Herbert Beaver,* ed. Thomas E. Jessett. Champoeg Press, Portland OR 1959, pp. 36-7.

7. *The Letters of John McLoughlin, Second Series 1839-44,* ed. E.E. Rich. Hudson's Bay Record Society, London 1943, p. 2.

8. Company fines, in the form of withheld wages, are mentioned several times in letters by Simpson, McLoughlin and others. See *Simpson's Athabasca Journal,* ed. E.E. Rich, (London: The Hudson's Bay Record Society, 1938), pp. 398-99. The Company's disciplinary control over its employees also is described by Gray, p. 196, above.

9. Minutes of the Council of Northern Department of Rupert's Land. Hudson's Bay Record Society, London 1940, p. 133.

10. Simpson's journal, pp. 398-99.

11. "Diary of Wilkes in the Northwest," Edmond S. Meany. Washington Historical Quarterly, vol. 16, 1925, pp. 222-23.

12. McLoughlin letters, second series, pp. 307-08.

2.
"Let Him Shake and Be Damned."

McLoughlin had never had a jail before the 1840s because, apparently, he didn't think he needed one. But his status as an autocrat was under growing threat. He could no longer count on absolute obedience from every living soul anywhere within reach of Fort Vancouver. Americans were building their own community south of the Columbia River, threatening not just Hudson's Bay's authority but Britain's prospects for adding Oregon to the British Empire. Even so, McLoughlin was expected to run the Columbia Department at a profit and do it with the desperados that Simpson sent him.

For whatever reason—and the reason was never officially explained—McLoughlin built a jail. The structure simply appeared as a small building on a map of the fort about 1843-44. The building was unlabeled, but it occupied the spot where the jail is known to have existed. References to it began appearing in fort correspondence, but with no informative details. There was occasional mention that someone had been "prisoned," but this word was used before there actually was a jail, and likely meant that the culprit had been put in irons. Several letters in the 1820s and late 1830s made clear that actual "prisoning" was not an option at the time.[1] The word "confinement" was sometimes used, but appears to have meant that whoever was being confined was simply kept in some location under close supervision.

After shackling a seaman in 1826 for stealing rum from a Company ship, McLoughlin explained to headquarters that "we could not (as we have no prison) keep him in confinement unless we put him in irons."[2]

James "Black" Douglas, McLoughlin's adjutant, reported in 1838 that he'd sent four mutineers to other Company outposts to await deportation to England since there was no "convenient place" to incarcerate them at Fort Vancouver.[3]

Until there was a jail, lawbreakers at the Fort apparently were kept in the kitchen, with the cook assigned as keeper. Chaplain Beaver recounted the case of an employee who was chained up that way for more than five months after first receiving 40 lashes at the gun. The man's crime was "dereliction of duty," not otherwise described.[4]

Beaver said he pleaded with McLoughlin to let the man out of his chains because of illness, but that McLoughlin profanely refused. "During the continuance of it," wrote Beaver, "he (the prisoner) was attacked with intermittent fever, which being reported to the officer in charge of the establishment (McLoughlin), his reply was, " 'Let him shake and be damned.' "

Beaver said the cook felt sorry enough for the prisoner to remove his chains occasionally at the risk of having to take his place if he escaped.[5]

The prolonged use of shackles seems to have been a rarity at Fort Vancouver, however. Flogging was McLoughlin's preferred way of correcting anyone of the lower ranks who displeased him. The simple reason was that "prisoning" the offender in the kitchen kept him from labor that profited the Company.

Olivier Martineau, a voyageur and notorious skirt-chaser, drew a whipping for giving his blanket to a winsome Indian woman. "Martineau," fumed McLoughlin in a letter to headquarters, "is a Man who would give all his clothing to Women and leave himself naked so as to be unable to go out of the house and the other Men would have to do his duty."[6]

Corporal punishment undoubtedly occurred more often at Fort Vancouver and 34 outposts than the written record discloses. The outposts were not often visited by dignitaries who might have remarked on floggings in their correspondence, and those responsible for the floggings might not have been eager to advertise them.

The Rev. Gray, the American clergyman and writer who jotted down a description of the penal artillery parked at McLoughlin's front porch, stated in his *History of Oregon* that Fort Vancouver employees "by the articles of enlistment, were bound to obey all orders of a superior officer, as much so as a soldier in the army. Flogging was a common punishment (ordered) by all grades of officers, from a petty clerk of a trading post up to the governor of the company."[7]

Fort Vancouver's gentlemen residents almost never suffered the indignity of physical punishment. According to Chaplain Beaver, officers who drew McLoughlin's ire were merely confined to quarters.[8]

The only known flogging of a member of the Establishment occurred in 1837 when John Fisher Robinson, the fort's inebriate schoolmaster, was caught taking liberties with some of his girl pupils. One was the young daughter of acting chief trader, John Work. "Black" Douglas, who was temporarily in charge while McLoughlin was away, had Robinson flogged not just once but twice. Feelings ran so high at the fort that the quaking schoolmaster must have considered himself lucky not to be lynched.[9]

Many details about Fort Vancouver's robust penal practices might have been lost to history except for the busy pen of the Rev. Mister Beaver. Beaver's motive, of course, was not to assist historians but to avenge himself on McLoughlin. And he had the means to do it— namely the ear of Benjamin Harrison of London, deputy-governor of the Hudson's Bay Company.

Harrison was a recognized member of Britain's upper crust whose royal appointments had included chairmanship of the Exchequer Loan Board and as a liquidator of the South Sea Company. Better known today as the South Sea Bubble, it was a stock company Parliament created to reduce Britain's national debt. Promises of huge profits at little risk created a frenzy to buy stock, turning South Sea into a Ponzi scheme of historic proportions. It collapsed when new money stopped coming in, and even Isaac Newton lost his shirt.

Burying the remains of South Sea with a minimum further embarrassment to the British Establishment was a job entrusted only to insiders like Harrison, Beaver's patron.

When Rev. Beaver sailed into Vancouver in 1836, he brought along an ego exceeded only by a lack of common sense. His wife, Jane, soon was dubbed "Haughty Jane" because of her disdain for people at the fort she felt were not her social equal, which included nearly everybody. She was, in other words, the ideal match for her husband.

Inevitably, Vancouver proved not nearly big enough for McLoughlin and the new chaplain.

Things got off to a rocky start when McLoughlin removed Beaver from the Fort Vancouver school after discovering he was teaching his pupils a militant brand of Anglicanism. The pupils were mostly the children of French-Canadian fur trappers—half-wild backwoodsmen and nearly all Roman Catholic. Although few could be accused of piety, the old religion was bred in their bones and McLoughlin was afraid that one of them might just add Beaver's pelt to his collection.

McLoughlin explained this to Beaver, but the chaplain saw darker motives. He suspected McLoughlin of being a closet Catholic despite a late, career-enhancing conversion to Anglicanism. And Beaver may have been right.

Although McLoughlin had switched religions to help him climb the corporate ladder, he kept many ties with the Catholic Church. He welcomed visiting priests and encouraged them to administer the sacraments and preach Sunday sermons. He also remained close to his sister who was a nun in Canada.

Beaver's mistrust led to an outright feud. He wrote letters to London describing in lurid detail the floggings and other punishments McLoughlin handed out at Fort Vancouver. He claimed he was trying to protect employees from abuse, but his more transparent aim was to get McLoughlin fired.

The final straw came from his efforts to "improve morals" at the fort—the ostensible reason the Hudson's Bay Company had sent him to Oregon. Translated into English, it meant regularizing the many "fur-trade marriages" between Company employees and Native women.

But morals had little to do with it. What Beaver's appointment was about was the Company's business interests and the geopolitical concerns of the British Empire.

Pressuring employees to legally marry was a devious scheme Simpson invented to strengthen British claims to Oregon and thus preserve the Hudson's Bay Company's franchise. It depended on the threat posed by British criminal law regarding bigamy.

Here's how it worked: An Oregon boundary settlement between Great Britain and the United States was in the offing, and the biggest decider would be population numbers. The question would be how many Americans lived in Oregon vs. how many British. Simpson planned to overcome the obvious U.S. advantage by pressuring Hudson's Bay men to legally marry the Native women they lived with. Practically all were in "fur-trade marriages." Maneuvering the men to the altar would increase the number of British subjects rapidly by manufacturing them wholesale out of people already in Oregon.

But what difference would legal marriages make?

A big one.

It would give the men serious incentive to stay in Oregon at the end of their enlistments instead of deserting their fur-trade families and running back to Canada alone. A legally married man who deserted his wife and married another could be charged with Bigamy, a capital offense under Canadian and British law. A legally married man who didn't want to remain a lifelong bachelor would likely find it more appealing to stay in Oregon with his family than abscond and wed another woman and risk being hanged.

These marriages had produced astonishing numbers of offspring, so each marriage Rev. Beaver could regularize meant an appreciable uptick in British population. The number of British subjects in the territory would be bound to grow much faster than Americans could arrive by covered wagon.

Beaver was going all-out with his morality crusade when one of the irregular marriages he saw fit to criticize was McLoughlin's. And he did so in writing, in a letter to Governor Harrison. He described McLoughlin's half-Chippewa companion of 25 years as a "notoriously loose woman" whose behavior scandalized the fort. It was outrageous slander, not even close to the truth. John and Marguerite Wadin McLoughlin had lived happily and devotedly together as husband and wife all their adult lives. She was a plain, dumpy, good-hearted woman several years McLoughlin's senior, and he fairly doted on her. And woe to anyone who showed her the slightest disrespect.[10]

A copy of Rev. Beaver's letter fell into McLoughlin's hands, and his reaction was volcanic. He caught the meddlesome chaplain in the yard, grabbed him and threw him to ground, cursed him for a blackguard, kicked his rump and thrashed him with his own cane.[11]

Beaver's bruises soon healed, but he brooded at length over his public humiliation. "Of whites," he wrote, "none but those of the lowest rank have ever been subjected to personal violence. Had I received such a few years ago, I would hardly have now been alive; they (the Indians) would have thought they were doing a service in destroying me."[12]

He returned to England but continued to seek revenge. He wrote and published several sensational but basically accurate exposes of Fort Vancouver's harsh treatment of employees, blaming "the gentleman in charge of that establishment."[13]

Even if Beaver's motives were not the purest, he did bring some real abuses to light and, to his credit, didn't clearly invent or exaggerate them. He gave a well-deserved airing of the mistreatment of Sandwich Islanders (Hawaiians) who made up a good portion of Fort Vancouver's labor force.

Beaver said the Hawaiians' chiefs had been bribed to sign them over as indentured servants on the promise that the good-natured islanders would get double the usual pay of £17 per year. He said the Company did pay the double rate, but slyly recouped the money by overcharging the Hawaiians for subsistence items at the Company store.

"Their condition is little better than that of slavery, being subject to all the imperious treatment which their employees may think fit to lay on them, whether by flogging, imprisonment or otherwise, without a possibility of redress," Beaver reported.

I knew (a) Sandwich Islander to be severely flogged although bearing a general good character, for making a trifleing mistake, unattended by any injury to the service, with respect to some orders which he had received, and which, from his ignorance of the language in which they were conveyed, he probably had not understood. I knew another to die in the hospital, as was generally supposed, in consequences of a wound inflicted on his head by the commander of one of the Company's vessels. He was continually convulsed, having a sort of paralytic motion or catching of the head and neck.[14]

Beaver said another ship's captain informed him that a Hawaiian had died at sea in 1832, apparently from the effects of a severe flogging he got at Fort Vancouver for stealing a pig.[15]

One of the more sensational charges that Rev. Beaver flung at McLoughlin's administration was an accusation that the fort surgeon had punitively castrated a transvestite Indian. The Company found the charge difficult to deny because it was true. It took place in February 1835. That was nearly two years before Beaver arrived but the story was still circulating.

A Fort Vancouver visitor, the eccentric Hall Jackson Kelley, gave British authorities in the Sandwich Islands an affidavit describing the incident shortly after it occurred, but nothing was done about it. While Kelley could be written off as a crank, Beaver was an Establishment clergyman writing a letter published in a London newspaper.[16]

The embarrassed Company, fearing yet another attack from its critics in Parliament, already had asked for and received an accounting from McLoughlin, who excused himself from blame. He explained to the board:

> This Indian used to dress himself as a woman and go about the place and on board of the Vessel and annoy everyone he met, with his abominable proposals, and for which he had been repeatedly flogged by the people so as to drive him away but in spite of this after keeping away some time he would come back. The Doctor vexed at this Wretches conduct and without speaking to me on the subject got hold of him near the Hospital and with the assistance of some of the people emasculated him.[17]

McLoughlin said he chastised the physician, Dr. Meredith Gairdner, as soon as he heard of the incident. But he said he understood why Gairdner did what he did. "The doctor," McLoughlin explained, "was a man of strong religious feelings and...if he acted improperly in this instance it was from a horror of what was wrong, and a zeal to do what was right."

Whatever the board thought about Gairdner's handiwork, it was unable to order a reprimand because Gairdner had died meantime of tuberculosis. McLoughlin passed along one other excuse that Gairdner had offered for the castration—that he thought it more merciful than the death penalty which English criminal law prescribed for sodomy. McLoughlin said Gairdner assured him that he'd have "recommended the Wretch be hanged, had this situation occurred in England."[18]

After the stir caused by Beaver's letters died down, little more was said about the goings-on at Fort Vancouver. The cat-'o-nine-tails continued to be laid on as often as McLoughlin and other officials saw fit. Even after McLoughlin built a jail in about 1843-44, he continued to have men whipped.

Two Hawaiians were flogged at the gun and "put in confinement" in October 1844 for burgling a fort storeroom during confusion caused by a forest fire.

On August 19, 1846, a Canadian who tried twice to desert was given 13 lashes and "put in prison."[19]

Sometimes, minor offenders were treated with forbearance. Several employees who got so drunk they were unable to work were allowed to sober up in irons. One Isaac Labelle, a first-time deserter, was hunted down and marched back to the fort and thrown in jail until he posted bail.

Exactly why McLoughlin thought he needed a jail after having gotten along without one for so many years is a question for which there is no certain answer.

By the mid-1840s, Fort Vancouver had become a fair-sized community with surprisingly urbanized institutions. It had a circulating library, a fire department with a horse-drawn fire engine, two churches, a hospital, and a school. A jail might have been just one more ornament of civilized society.

Although the fort proper was basically just a 750x450 foot log stockade enclosing several acres of buildings and grounds, the community it accommodated both inside and outside the walls was less like a fur-trade outpost than a boiled-down version of New York City. Besides the English-speaking officials and clerks who ran the place, Fort Vancouver jostled with French-speaking trappers and voyageurs who also spoke Chinook trade jargon, Scottish farmers whose burred accents were as tangy as the apples they grew, Polynesian-speaking Hawaiian laborers, Scottish and Canadian artisans and craftsmen, Indians of several different tribes and dialects, and an occasional American or two. For a while, Fort Vancouver even had some Japanese residents—sailors who had survived a shipwreck.[20]

The stew of nationalities and ethnicities was more than just colorful. It made for a complex legal situation. Different laws applied to different groups with some applying to British subjects and others to non-British Europeans, and a mishmash of laws and regulations for Company employees of whatever nationality, and still others for visiting Americans, Native Americans, and a shifting cast of visitors.

Serious lawbreaking was rare but when it did occur not every perpetrator could be safely flogged or even interfered with. So a jail standing at the ready would have given McLoughlin an appearance of sovereign authority even if he couldn't always do what he wanted.

In simpler times, before Americans began settling in Oregon in significant numbers and diluting his imperium, McLoughlin had had little need to ponder the finer points of law. He just did whatever he thought was right, or at least necessary. It blended perfectly with the Hudson's Bay Company's own imperial style.

For many years before it expanded into Oregon, the Company had run what amounted to its own independent country in central Canada. Rupert's Land, so-called, was created in 1670 by King Charles II of England for his favorite cousin and tennis partner, Prince Rupert, who wanted to enter the fur trade with some cronies. Charles granted Rupert and his pals a royal charter dubbing them "The Governor and

Company of Adventurers of England Tradeing Into Hudson's Bay." For all practical purposes, it was title to a large part of North America and everybody in it.[21]

The Hudson's Bay Company was to have

> sole Trade and Commerce of all those Seas Streights Bayes Rivers Lakes Creekes and Sounds in whatsoever Latitude they shall bee that lay within the entrance of the Streights commonly called Hudsons Streights together with all the Lands Countryes and Territoryes upon the Coasts and Confynes of the Seas Streights Bayes Lakes Rivers Creekes and Sounds aforesaid which are not now actually possessed by any of our Subjects or by the Subjects of any other Christian Prince or State.

Maps in those days being imprecise, Charles had only the roughest idea of what he was giving away. It was supposed to be the Hudson Bay basin. But as time went on, the Company claimed most of present-day Canada between the bay and the Rocky Mountains. Oregon wound up in the Company's pocket much later although it was not part of Charles's original grant.[22]

The way the royal charter read the Company was more than just the practical owner of a lot of real estate. Its rights of possession were expressed in nearly biblical terms, like the title to Eden that Adam got from Jehovah. The Company's leaders and their successors were declared "true and absolute lords and proprietors." They could, in the words of the charter,

> make ordeyne and constitute such and soe many reasonable lawes, constitucions orders and ordinances as the governor and Company shall deeme necessary for the good government of the colony." They also could "lawfully impose, ordeyne, limitt and provyde such paines, penalties and punishments upon all offenders as the majority and governor deeme fit.

The charter allowed the Company to delegate to its North American representatives the "power to judge all persons belonging to the (Company), or that shall live under them, in all causes, whether civil or criminal, according to the laws of the kingdom, and to execute justice accordingly."

It said that,

> in case any crime or misdemeanor shall be committed in any of the said Company's plantations, forts, factories or places of trade within the limits aforesaid, where judicature cannot be executed for want of a Governor and Council there, then in such case it shall and may be lawful for the chief factor of that place and his Council to transmit the party, together with the offence, to such other plantations, factory or fort where there shall be a Governor and council, where justice may be executed, or into this Kingdom of England, as shall be thought most convenient, and there to receive such punishment as the nature of his offense shall deserve.

The charter also let the Company discipline unsatisfactory employees. Company officers could "inflict punishment for misdemeanors, or impose fines upon [employees] for breach of their orders."[23]

In summary, the inhabitants of Rupert's Land were subject to three kinds of law under the royal charter: British criminal and civil law; Hudson's Bay Company laws, if any were formally enacted; and Company disciplinary rules that could be made up on the spot and might vary from post to post.

As for any Native peoples the Company encountered, the charter provided the option of extermination. It allowed the Company to "make peace or Warre with any Prince or People whatsoever that are not Christians."

Yet, having given the Company a great deal of administrative flexibility, to say the least, the King cautioned that it not run amok. The charter expected the Company to govern "in a legall and reasonable manner" and that any laws the Company might pass "bee reasonable and not contrary or repugnant but as near as may bee agreeable to the lawes, statutes or customes of this Realme." In other words, Charles was telling the Company to act properly, and in case of doubt to do the right thing. The King would judge what had been right.

With its ambiguities and near-contradictions, the royal charter was a small masterpiece of Seventeenth Century British legal construction. What it lacked in clarity it made up for in uncertainty—not a bad thing in a system without a written constitution. As Charles no doubt intended, the Hudson's Bay Company never was absolutely sure what its charter allowed, and therefore resolved any doubts by behaving cautiously.

John Nixon, an early Company governor of Rupert's Land, discovered the charter's limits when he sought in 1682 to maintain authority over rebellious subordinates. It seems that the drunken captain of a Company ship had invited Nixon publicly to "kiss his arse," annoying Nixon so greatly that he wrote to London asking the board's leave to hang the man for impertinence.

Company policy was to return serious offenders to England for trial, but Nixon argued that discipline would soon disappear entirely if he had to follow such rigamarole. He suggested that a writ of martial law would clear up any doubts about his authority to impose the death penalty as circumstances required. Although the charter didn't say specifically that the Company could use martial law, he pointed out, it didn't forbid it, either. And since martial law was a part of British law, it could be emulated by the Company, Nixon argued.

> If I could avoyd, I would not pass sentance of death on any man, but the crime being such, as that by a counsell we may prove the fact against a criminall, according to the booke of articles in that casse provyded, and accordingly chastise him with corporall punishment for ane example to others, or else send him home in irons to receave his punishment in England.[24]

One can only imagine the thoughts that passed through the heads of the Company owners as they sat in London reading Nixon's request. Although the charter described them as a "company of adventurers," they were more accurately a bunch of nervous businessmen in tea-doily wigs, none very anxious to risk the royal franchise to salve Nixon's pride.

They let his request die quietly on the vine.

Although the royal charter might have allowed the Company to hang employees if proper procedures were followed, it didn't authorize government by whim. When the sea-captain made his insulting remark to Nixon, the Company had not yet used its legislative powers to pass laws of any kind in Rupert's Land. This meant there was no law in effect there except the laws of England. Moreover, the Company couldn't have passed a law allowing it to hang someone for sassing his boss, since there was no such offense in the English criminal code.[25]

The fact of the matter is that the Hudson's Bay Company never was greatly interested in making laws, capital or otherwise, because there was no profit in it. The Company was a business owned by absentee stockholders who wanted to make money. Although the charter referred to Rupert's Land as a "colony," it was never really that. It was more of a commercial zone. Its inhabitants were mostly Company employees, and its posts and settlements were company towns. A worker who got out of line could simply be beaten or his wages withheld. Anything more elaborate would have been inconvenient and an unnecessary expense. Still, the Company by 1682, was presenting itself as more than just a business. It flew a company flag—a red and white ensign with a big "HBC" logo. In 1707 it changed this to a slightly modified Union Jack. However, an HBC logo was prominent on all three.

The Company's reluctance to distract itself with government-like activities, despite the flag fetish, continued for 165 years. It was not until 1835 that the Company exercised its right under the royal charter to pass actual laws for Rupert's Land.[26]

It was more or less forced to. The trigger was a backwoods war over beaver pelts.

2. NOTES

1. Fort Vancouver Historic Structures Report. John A. Hussey. U.S. National Park Service, 1972. Manuscript copy of chapter 21, pp. 436-37.

2. McLoughlin letter cited by Hussey, p. 436.

3. *Hudson's Bay Company Correspondence Book,* Fort Vancouver 1838, HBC Archives, b.223/b/21, ms. 92-94; Correspondence Book, Fort Vancouver, 1838-39, Hudson's Bay Archives, b.223/b/22, ms, fols. 4-4d, 5d-6, cited by Hussey in historic structures manuscript, p. 438, above.

4. Herbert Beaver's "Letter to the Aborigines Protection Society of London," Tract No. 8, 1842, cited by Nellie B. Pipes in "Indian Conditions in Oregon 1836-38," *Oregon Historical Quarterly*, vol. 32, 1931, p. 340.

5. Cited by Jessett, p. 86.

6. McLoughlin's letters, 2nd series, p. 364.

7. Gray, p. 196.

8. Jessett, p. 76.

9. Francis Ermatinger letter to his brother, Edward, Feb. 26, 1839. Huntington Library, San Marino, Calif. HM 16761. Robinson also is mentioned in a letter from Herbert Beaver to William Cameron McKay, May 27, 1840. University of Oregon Library Special Collections, William Cameron McKay Papers (MF 27.)

10. Douglas wrote of McLoughlin's attitude toward Marguerite, "Though his wife was a half-breed of the Ojibway nation, coarse, bent, fat and flabby, he treated her like a princess. In public and in private he was as loyal to her as if she had been a daughter of Queen Victoria...He would suffer no indignity or slight to her. His fine handsome form beside the uncorseted figure of the old Indian woman presented a strange contrast, as she waddled beside him like a being of another species." Cited by Derek Pethick, *James Douglas: Servant of Two Empires*. Mitchell Press Ltd. Vancouver, 1969, pp. 23-24.

11. Beaver letter to HBC governor and committee Oct. 10, 1837, HBC correspondence book HBC archives b. 223/b/19, fos. 9d. and 10d., cited

by ed. E.E. Rich in *The Letters of John McLoughlin, Third Series 1844-46* (London: Champlain Society for HBRS, 1944), p. cxx. Also see p. 102 of Beaver's Reports cited by Jessett. Probably the most entertaining overview of the Beaver-McLoughlin feud is in Malcolm Clark Jr.'s uproarously readable history of Oregon's settlement, *Eden Seekers*. Houghton Mifflin, Boston 1981, pp. 111-13.

12. Jessett, p. 102.

13. Ibid.

14. Beaver's "Letter to the Aborigines Protection Society of London," cited by Pipes, p. 341.

15. Ibid.

16. Beaver's letter, p. 337, above.

17. *Hudson's Bay Miscellaney*, ed. Glyndour Williams. Hudson's Bay Record Society, Winnipeg 1975, pp. 280-81.

18. Ibid.

19. Hussey, p. 439-40.

20. Document: "17th Anniversary Report, Methodist Annual Reports Relating to the Willamette Mission (1834-48)" ed. Charles H. Carey, *Oregon Historical Quarterly*, vol. 23, p. 307.

21. Horace Harvey. "Some Notes on the Early Administration of Justice in Canada's North-West." *The Pioneer West*, p. 12. Reprinted from *Alberta Historical Review*, November 1953 and January 1954. Harvey was chief justice of the Appellate Division of the Supreme Court of Alberta in 1924-49, and this densely-packed 20-page article provides a rare overview of criminal law enforcement during Company times.

22. The antique spellings are from a transcript of the surviving portion of Charles II's "Charter incorporating the Hudson's Bay Company, 2nd May 1670," courtesy of Hudson's Bay House Library, Winnipeg.

23. Whatever the charter meant, the Company certainly did use criminal justice methods to enforce discipline against its employees both within and without Rupert's Land. This is made clear by Company correspondence that openly discusses punishment for infractions that were obviously rule violations

rather than crimes. For instance, the flogging of Olivier Martineau for giving away his blanket.

24. *Minutes of the Hudson's Bay Company 1679-82,* 1st series. Hudson's Bay Record Society, London 1945, pp. 272-73.

25. The charter required the Company to keep its laws as similar as possible to England's. English law made mutiny a capital crime, and Nixon argued mildly that Captain Walker's insult had amounted to mutiny. However, no Company statute had been adopted prior to the alleged offense, and the captain would have had to be charged under English law, had the Company chosen to pursue the matter, which it didn't.

26. Harvey, p. 13. op. cit.

3.
Beaver fever

The discovery of a fabulous new source of beaver had drawn Hudson's Bay out of its franchised territory and into up-for-grabs Oregon. The new wilderness fairly swarmed with the busy rodents that were as irresistible to fur trappers as gold nuggets would be to the Forty-Niners of the California Gold Rush. In fact, beaver pelts were so valuable at one point that they were used as a medium of exchange. On the London market they turned an ungodly profit because no gentleman of any account could be seen in public without a tall beaver hat. To stroll the boulevard or call at one's club without a beaver stovepipe on one's noggin was unthinkable. The very costliness of the hat was one of its main attractions, publicly advertising the wearer's wealth.

The Columbia River drainage and its abundance of beaver made it a veritable Klondike, an El Dorado, a Lost Dutchman gold mine of the furry species Castor canadensis.

A war to dominate the market broke out in 1779 when a group of Canadian entrepreneurs formed the North West Company and began competing with the Company for furs. North West trappers couldn't enter Rupert's Land legally because of the Hudson's Bay Company's exclusive rights but were legally free to trap in the adjacent Indian territories. That mainly meant Oregon where the Hudson's Bay Company also operated, but without monopoly privileges.

The rivalry turned savage. There were killings and shootings and Indian agitations, all of which finally convinced the British Parliament to extend Canadian criminal law into the Indian territories although it wasn't clear by what authority it did so. The territories were a jurisdictional no-man's-land covered by no specific laws. A crime committed there might involve citizens of several different nations, raising the question of what they could be charged with and who would charge them. And who could even arrest them?

Parliament on Aug. 11, 1803, created a new statute, 40 George III, Chapter 138, labeling it "an act for extending the jurisdiction of the courts of justice in the provinces of Lower and Upper Canada, to the trial and punishment of persons guilty of crimes and offences within certain parts of North America adjoining to the said provinces."

The law declared simply that any further crimes in the territories would be treated as if they occurred in Ontario or Quebec. But this was complicated by the fact that the two provinces had substantially dissimilar legal systems—Ontario's being modeled after Britain's while Quebec's, in deference to its large French population, was patterned after France's.[1]

The administrative procedure spelled out by the new statute was a bit complicated also. The governor of Quebec was directed to appoint justices of the peace in the territories who would have the authority to arrest criminal suspects and return them to Canada for trial. The Quebec courts would have original jurisdiction in all cases, but the governor could change it to Ontario whenever appropriate.[2]

In 1809, a posse from the North West Company demanded and received custody of a man named Mowatt, a Hudson's Bay employee who was accused of shooting and killing a Mr. Macdonnell of the North West Company. Mowatt was put in irons and taken to Montreal where he was tried, convicted of manslaughter, and sentenced to six months' imprisonment and to be branded on the hand with a hot iron. In 1816, the Hudson's Bay Company's investigation of a multiple murder led it to arrest several North West Company employees, including none other than John McLoughlin. The future Fort Vancouver potentate was working at the time for North West.

McLoughlin and the rest were accused of complicity in the massacre of personnel at a Hudson's Bay Company post on the Red

River. The suspects were packed off to Quebec to face trial but the provincial governor changed the venue to Ontario where, two years later, McLoughlin and his fellow defendants were acquitted.[3]

Surprisingly, the 1803 statute permitted British agents to arrest foreigners as well as British subjects in the Indian territories. However, recognizing the problems such arrests might cause, the statute also required automatic acquittal, regardless of the evidence, for any suspect who was a citizen of the United States or any recognized European country.[4] It was a slick way to take a perp out of circulation for an extended period while British officials took their sweet time bringing the case to trial.

In the case of Mowatt and John McLoughlin and his associates, it may be worth noting that they were extradited from the Indian territories close to Rupert's Land and not from more distant Oregon. There is no record that anyone during this period was extradited from Oregon.

Practically speaking, the 1803 statute was more of a scarecrow than a law since there was no regular means of enforcing it. Although Quebec's governor could appoint temporary constables to arrest suspects in the unorganized territories, just about the only people who would be available for appointment would be the same fur traders whose rumpuses might make an appointment necessary.[5]

Needless to say, the fur wars continued largely unabated. When relief finally came, it was not through better laws and law enforcement, but through eliminating the source of the violence, which was commercial competition.

Parliament ended it in 1821 by enacting 1&2 George IV, Chapter 66, titled "An Act for regulating the Fur Trade and establishing a Criminal and Civil Jurisdiction within certain parts of North America." The lengthy and complex statute forced a merger of the two principal culprits, the Hudson's Bay Company and the North West Company. More precisely, Hudson's Bay was required to swallow its smaller rival. Also, the statute clarified and streamlined the way Canadian law would extend into the backcountry.[6]

By discouraging homicide in the woods, Parliament likely was less concerned about the welfare of the battling fur traders than about

British imperial ambitions in Oregon. Britain's claim to the vast Oregon country was being challenged by an upstart United States. In 1818, the two countries had acknowledged a standoff by signing a treaty agreeing that Oregon would remain open to occupancy by both sides for 10 years.

Britain used the time to bolster its case for permanent possession. The fur-trade companies' long presence in Oregon had given Britain a temporary advantage, but it was obvious that this would come to naught unless conditions were made right for civil society to take root. And that required a real upgrade to law and order.[7]

The Hudson's Bay Company's dominance before 1844-45 came with responsibilities forcing it to act like a government whether it wanted to or not. It had a legal obligation to enforce British and Canadian law.

The 1821 Fur Trade Act said the laws of Ontario would apply to crime, but preserved the Company's right to discipline its own employees as it saw fit. It was a legal arrangement remarkable for its intrusiveness since virtually every non-Indian in Oregon was on the Company payroll. So nearly everyone in Oregon old enough to walk was liable to both Canadian criminal law and Company whim.

> The Fur Trade Act required the Bay to post a surety bond guaranteeing it would carry out "the due Execution of all Processes criminal and civil" and see to "the producing or delivering into safe Custody, for Purpose of Trial, of all Persons in their Employ or acting under their authority, who shall be charged with any Criminal Offence, and also for the due and faithful Observance of all such Rules, Regulations and Stipulations as shall be contained in [the Royal charter] either for diminishing or preventing the Sale or Distribution of Spiritous Liquors to the Indians, or for promoting their moral and religious improvement, or for any other Object which his Majesty may deem necessary for the Remedy or Prevention of the other Evils which have hitherto been found to exist.[8]

So even the Indians didn't escape completely.

Although fur-trade Justices were appointed technically by the Crown, they were inevitably Company officers and could be counted on to see things from the Company's point of view. And their authority was considerable.

They could "sit and hold Courts of Record for the Trial of Criminal Offences and Misdemeanors," except for felonies, "made the Subject of Capital Punishment, or for any Offence or passing Sentence affecting the life of any offender, or adjudge or cause any Offender to suffer Capital Punishment, or Transportation [to a penal colony]."

The law went on to say that

> in every case of any Offence subjecting the person committing the same to Capital Punishment or Transportation, the Court of any Judge of any such Court, or any Justice or Justices of the Peace before whom any Offender shall be brought, shall commit such Offender to safe Custody, and cause such Offenders to be sent in such Custody for Trial in the Court of the Province of Upper Canada [Ontario].[9]

The Ontario criminal laws that the 1821 Fur Trade Act had extended into Oregon had been transplanted from England just a short while earlier, in 1800. They had been scattered here and there in 40 George III, chapter 1. By adopting 40 George, British parliament gave Ontario and its predominantly British settlers virtually the entire English criminal law as it stood Sept. 17, 1792.[10]

Parliament may or may not have understood exactly what it was sending the Canadians. Unlike the criminal laws of the United States, those of England had never been codified systematically but were scribbled onto the books as Parliament thought of them, in no particular order. A law prescribing the death penalty for cutting down a cherry tree in an orchard might follow a law taxing the import of Italian crepe, and precede a law regulating coal mining in Wales.

Thus, the English criminal statutes that were shipped to Oregon by way of Ontario resembled, in organizational style, an unsorted collection of laundry tickets.

Among the approximately 200 hanging offenses to be found there, with sufficient patience, were several curiosities that Parliament might have donated more appropriately to a wax museum. It was punishable by death under 40 George to travel through a forest without blowing a horn, to steal a sheep, to shoplift an article worth more than five shilling, to imagine the death of the King, to appear on a public roadway wearing a disguise, or to be seen for a month in the company of "persons who call themselves, or are called, Egyptians."[11]

Not surprisingly, a good many English judges by the mid-19th Century thought some of the laws were ridiculous and refused to enforce them. But not every judge felt free to do so, and occasionally there was an atrocious execution.[12]

Revisions in the law gave Canadian judges some discretion as to the details of punishment. Except for manslaughter cases, judges could substitute floggings or "moderate fines" for the old English penalty of branding felons on the hand with a hot iron.[13]

The revisionist authors, apparently afraid they'd be scorned as softies, went to some length to justify themselves. They pointed out that branding had largely fallen into disuse anyway because most judges were reluctant to order it. The judges, they said, felt that branding was not only cruel but also counterproductive because it "fixed a lasting mark of disgrace and infamy on offenders, who might otherwise become good subjects and profitable members of the community." Since branding had thus ceased being a credible deterrent, the lawmakers said, some other kind of penalty was needed to take its place.

But in typical British fashion, the authors fudged a bit so that their new version didn't absolutely forbid judges to have criminals branded if they thought it justified. Or they could order a lashing. Or both a lashing and a branding. If a lashing was ordered, the culprit could be

> once, or oftener, but not more than three times, either publicly or privately whipt; such private whipping to be inflicted in the presence of not less than two persons besides the offender and the officer who inflicts the same; and in case of female offenders, in the presence of females only.[14]

A public whipping was considered worse punishment than a private one because it added humiliation to pain. Although the maximum number of whippings allowed by statute was three, nothing was said about the number of strokes per session.

Whether all the fudging and hemming and hawing made the original law less or more atrocious is hard to say.

Finally, the transmittal statute was careful to emphasize that corporal punishments or fines needn't substitute entirely for imprisonment—that all three could be used together. But there was no question of allowing lawbreakers to loll about in prison for an extended period at public expense. The longest prison term allowed was two years, with corporal punishment and fines deployable to close the misery gap.

Nor should it be forgotten that a really serious offender could still be hanged or transported to a penal colony or banished if proper procedures were followed.

Banishment meant ordering someone to leave a certain place for a term ranging up to life. Depending on circumstances, the consequences ranged from inconvenience and loss of reputation, to death. Without community support and protection, a banished individual in certain situations could die of starvation, exposure to the elements, or from other causes such as enemy attack. Returning prematurely from banishment was a capital crime.[15]

The Hudson's Bay Company decided belatedly, in 1835, to shore up its unique status in Rupert's Land by creating a colonial government.

Using the 165-year-old charter as its authority, the Company appointed a 15-member Legislature that could do double-duty as a court. When acting in a judicial capacity it was dubbed "the Supreme Tribunal the Court of Governor and Council of Assiniboia."[16] This grand-sounding Company court functioned for some 30 years, although its legitimacy was suspect. Edmund Burke Wood, first chief justice of the Manitoba's Court of Queen's Bench, noted in 1872 that the Tribunal's authority had "rested upon the powers conferred on the Company by the charter granted in the reign of King Charles II, but on no legislative enactment whatever."

Despite this, said Wood, the Tribunal hadn't hesitated to empanel juries and try civil cases

> to any amount whatever and exercising criminal jurisdiction even to the extent of inflicting capital punishment [for in one instance at least one person was tried for murder, convicted and executed], without its basis or jurisdiction ever having been formally and authoritatively questioned by the Imperial Government.

Thus the fog continued as to the Company's legal footing outside Rupert's Land.

When James Calder, a Hudson's Bay employee, killed a co-worker on the Peace River, the Tribunal asked its legal adviser whether it could try the case. The adviser, one Adam Thom, wrote a tortuous brief saying he thought it could but he wasn't sure. Thom's opinion was based on a creative reading of geography as applied to the 1670 Royal Charter. The charter required the Company to look for an Arctic sea route to China—the fabled Northwest Passage—which Thom said gave the Company jurisdiction over the Peace since the Peace flowed into the Arctic Ocean.

The problem with Thom's argument was that it wasn't exactly true. The Peace River originated in the Canadian Rockies and flowed into the MacKenzie, which originated at Great Slave Lake. It was like saying the Ohio was really the Mississippi, a perilous reed to lean on if someone brought a charge of wrongful prosecution.

The Supreme Tribunal was not unduly impressed by Thom's opinion. After some dithering it adopted a resolution—to whom it was addressed wasn't clear—recommending that it be given authority to try Calder if it didn't already have it. Nothing came of the request.[17]

The Hudson's Bay Company's bobbing-and-weaving in the Peace River case was not uncharacteristic. Unless its commercial well-being was directly at stake, the Company sought to avoid rather than embrace governmental duties. In fact, the Company's refusal to prosecute a notorious murder case at an outpost far outside Rupert's Land may have led John McLoughlin to build Oregon's first jail.

McLoughlin had a personal stake because the victim was one of his sons, John McLoughlin Jr. The young man was shot and killed by subordinates at Fort Stikine in southwest Alaska, in April 1842.

The incident raised all sorts of jurisdictional questions. It not only occurred in Russian Alaska but it was on property the Company leased from the Russian government and involved suspects and witnesses of several different nationalities.

The muddle became a mess when Sir George Simpson, no fan of McLoughlin, started meddling. He produced statements from witnesses that John Jr. himself was to blame by getting drunk and bellicose and threatening employees who said they had to shoot him in self-defense.[18]

McLoughlin would have none of it.

He blamed Simpson for putting his son in jeopardy by giving him duties he wasn't prepared for. Simpson had left John Jr. in charge while he and the outpost manager were away on a business trip. It left the young man alone with some tough characters who ended up killing him. What really happened was never clear.

Getting no help from Simpson, the senior McLoughlin waged a long, lonely, grief-stricken campaign to wring justice from the Company. He asked the board of governors to petition the Russians to take charge of the case. The board sent a request through diplomatic channels to the Russian government in St. Petersburg as McLoughlin had the three prime suspects—Urbain Heroux, Pierre Kanaquasse, and Francoise Presse—delivered to Russia's Alaska headquarters at Sitka.

While waiting for the Tsarist government to respond, McLoughlin ordered that a dozen potential witnesses be detained at different Hudson's Bay outposts in the region—presumably to make sure they'd be available for a trial and to keep them separated so they couldn't coordinate their stories.

Simpson was furious when he heard what McLoughlin was doing. He dashed off a note ordering him to "no longer employ the hon. Company's servants & waste the hon. Company's resources" preparing for a trial that Simpson was sure would be futile even if it occurred. He pointed to witness statements already in hand describing the killing as justified. This version of events would, of course, excuse Simpson from a career-damaging lapse in judgment for giving McLoughlin Jr. a job he couldn't handle.

The Russian government sent word declining to get involved. Its official excuse was that it lacked jurisdiction because the Company held Fort Stikine under treaty.

When news of the decision reached McLoughlin and a few close friends in the fall of 1843, they were sure the Russians were just trying to duck responsibility. One of McLoughlin's friends suggested slipping the Russians at Fort Stikine a little money to ship the suspects to an uncertain fate in Siberia.[19]

Nothing came of it.

McLoughlin pressed on for a trial before the Supreme Tribunal, and sent a posse of lieutenants to collect the suspects from Sitka and round up witnesses and march them south to Fort Vancouver. The party wintered at the fort before going on to Rupert's Land and what McLoughlin hoped would be a trial the following spring. He sent along documents including a letter to his lawyer in Montreal instructing him to prosecute privately if neither the Company nor the Canadian authorities would do so.[20]

By now, McLoughlin's insistence on the guilt of men who had been exonerated by all known witnesses was starting to worry even his friends. They were afraid a father's natural grief had blinded him to the possible legal consequences of what he was doing.

Counselor Thom added to the alarm by writing a legal opinion, at Simpson's request, outlining the technical obstacles to prosecuting the diverse group McLoughlin had sent to Canada. Thom's original document has since been lost, but Simpson forwarded a summary to London headquarters on June 21, 1844. It read:

> With reference to the prisoners and witnesses alluded to in the foregoing para., Mr. Chief Factor McLoughlin has sent across two men to be tried on the charge of

having murdered the late Mr. John McLoughlin as also
eleven witnesses and an interpreter, the prisoners being
respectively a Canadian [Heroux] and an Iroquois
[Kanaquasse] and the witnesses consisting of one Scotchman,
two Kanaccas and eight Canadians and Iroquois.

In this unfortunate case, we have had to contend with
the most serious perplexities, both legal & practical;
and on each of those two heads I shall briefly submit
to your honors the result of our deliberations.

His ensuing memo expanded on Thom's legal arguments against pursuing the case—and took some new shots at McLoughlin.

To begin with the legal aspect of the case, Mr. [Recorder]
Thom seems to be clearly of the opinion that Canada has
no jurisdiction beyond the [Rocky] mountains and is
inclined to think that, though England Proper may take
cognizance of the charges under the letter of 9 Geo. 4. Ch.
31, S.7,9,[21] yet even her jurisdiction may have been rendered
inconsistent with the spirit of the statute by the proceedings
in Russia. But further, even if the jurisdiction, as such, were
not a subject of doubt, it could not possibly extend to any
other than British subjects; and Mr. Thom would suggest
that in all probability the Iroquois prisoner [Kanaquasse]
might not be considered a British Subject according to the
liberal & indulgent principles of penal interpretation.

In addition to this view of the position of the prisoners,
Mr. Thom points out the illegality and injustice of sending
the witnesses, particularly the Scotchman and the Kanaccas,
to Canada against their own inclination, till they shall be
regularly summoned under the statute. From all these
premises, that gentleman recommended as the best practical
course, that the prisoners should be permitted to pass onward
under the original authority, and that the witnesses should
be disposed of merely in their capacity as servants. But here
arose our practical perplexities. With regard to the prisoners,
Mr. Chief Factor McLoughlin had not forwarded any warrant
so as to justify the necessary restraint during the downward
voyage; and after much consideration, we saw no other course
before us than that of sending the two men to Montreal as
retiring servants and of intimating their arrival at Lachine to
the Honorable George Moffatt, whom Mr. McLoughlin in the

event of our declining to act in the matter, has authorised to conduct the prosecution in his name and on his responsibility.

With regard again to the witnesses, whose wages excepting those of the two Kanaccas, had all been withheld on the alleged ground of a conspiracy to murder, a ground which Mr. McLoughlin himself has practically abandoned, we necessarily decided that all arrears should be paid; and we further resolved, that the Kanaccas should be sent back to the Columbia, that the Scotchman, whose period of service had expired, should have the option of going home by York Factory or of remaining under a renewed contract on this side the mountains and that such of the Canadians and Iroquois as had completed their engagements, should be obliged to return to their own country as retiring servants.

In the whole case our aim has been to assume as little responsibility as possible and at the same time to facilitate the prosecution by every means not incompatible with the rights and feelings of innocent parties. Neither by this course, nor by any other practicable course, can the Hudsons Bay Company expect to avoid popular censure in this most untoward business; and if, as I firmly believe, the prisoners either escape unpunished or receive at most a trifling punishment, Mr. McLoughlin will hardly find in his own feelings any compensation for the odium which he will have heaped, and the injury which he will have inflicted, on the honorable company. Your honors will see, that I have requested Mr. McLoughlin to make up a statement of all the expences of the investigation, so that your honors may be able to decide whether the burden is to fall on the Fur trade or on Mr. McLoughlin himself.[22]

Historian John Hussey, an authority on Fort Vancouver's buildings, has speculated that John McLoughlin built the jail as a transit station for the suspects and witnesses he sent east in 1844. There was no mention of it in Fort records, but the time bracket can be established in other ways. George Foster Emmons, a visiting American, drew a site map on July 25, 1841 that didn't show a jail, but a small building occupying the jail's known location appeared in a September 1844 sketch by Henry N. Peers, a Fort clerk.[23]

The fact that the jail popped up without fanfare just as McLoughlin was transporting men to Canada to stand trial for his son's murder seems unlikely to be a coincidence.

Regardless of exactly when or why McLoughlin built his jail, quite a bit can be said about it. In 1950, National Park Service archaeologists excavated the jail's remains near the north wall of the Fort and discovered footings for a structure measuring 22x20 feet. Based on Peers' sketch and what is known about construction at the fort at that time, Hussey believed the jail was single-story and likely made of thick, hand-hewn timbers, with a peaked roof covered with wooden shakes. The longer side of the jail, as revealed by the footings, was parallel to the north wall of the Fort. The entry most likely was a solid wooden door with a padlock and perhaps a peep-hole.[24]

Edouard "Frenchy" Chambreau, who spent time in the jail in December 1848, penciled the only known eyewitness account in an unpublished autobiography more than 30 years later. He mentioned that whoever dropped files into the jail to help him cut through "le chaine" had spoken to him through an air-hole.

"I could not see who it was that spoke to me," Chambreau remembered. "The two air-holes of the jail were about eight feet from the floor."

Chambreau's reference to "air-holes" makes it pretty clear that the jail had no windows. And possibly there was no peep-hole in the door, either. If there had been, and the door faced the yard, it may not have been wise for his helpers to deliver the files that way because of the danger of being seen. The air-holes evidently were too small to crawl through, and they couldn't be reached anyway because they were too high off the floor. Chambreau noted that he had to wait until Old Bruce, the jailer, opened the door to deliver breakfast before he could complete his escape.[25]

"Old Bruce" undoubtedly was William Bruce, a longtime menial laborer and gardener who also worked as a kitchen assistant. Bruce's combination of culinary and penal duty was a common arrangement both before and after the jail was built. One of Bruce's co-workers tended a fettered prisoner in the kitchen before the jail existed.[26]

Not a lot is known about Bruce. He was a bachelor who had fled Scotland in disgrace as a bankrupt many years earlier. Once during his long tenure with the Company, he quit and went back to Scotland. But he soon returned to Fort Vancouver and resumed his old jobs tending the garden, helping in the kitchen and fetching McLoughlin's snuff. The Christmas he was knocked in the head by Frenchy Chambreau turned out to be his last. He died eight months later, August 25, 1849.[27]

Although Bruce apparently was Oregon's very first jailer, it's uncertain whether he also delivered floggings. But there is evidence that corporal punishment was one of the side-chores of the kitchen staff, in addition to jailing.

Beaver mentioned in his report on the William Brown flogging that it was done by a mess steward. Beaver didn't name him but said he was "clumsy" and "left-handed." That could have been almost anyone, since the Fort's personnel assignment lists were seldom precise. The only person specifically identified as working in the kitchen around the time of Brown's flogging was William Burris, a Londoner who served variously as a cook and steward in 1839-40 and 1842-43. Later, Burris settled in the Willamette Valley where he went berserk one day and killed his wife and children.[28]

Anyone unlucky enough to be lodged in the Fort Vancouver jail had to put up with several inconveniences, only one of which was being attached to "le chaine." The jail wasn't heated and was surely uncomfortable in winter. But that didn't keep it from being used. Chambreau's Christmas sojourn demonstrated as much.

To be fair to McLoughlin, Chambreau's incarceration in chilly December took place after James ("Black") Douglas took over as chief factor in 1845. McLoughlin seems to have been a little more considerate, sending two prisoners to winter at Fort Nisqually in October 1844 rather than lock them up in Vancouver.

"It would not do to keep them in a building without fire," McLoughlin explained in a note to his manager at Nisqually, "and all our buildings being of wood, they might be malicious enough to set them on fire."[29]

Except for "le chaine" and the absence of a fireplace, nothing else definite is known about the jail's amenities. Hussey noted that "rough wooden bunks, without springs or mattresses, were standard at Fort Vancouver," making it unlikely that anything more luxurious was afforded prisoners.

"A single blanket would have been considered sufficient bedding," he said.[30]

A few more details about the jail can be deduced from Chambreau's description of Bruce serving breakfast. Obviously it was dark inside, since Bruce didn't realize at once that Chambreau had gotten loose.

The fact that Bruce lay prone in the doorway to push Chambreau's food forward tells us that the chain was long enough to allow a prisoner some movement, but short enough to keep the jailer out of reach as long as he stayed near the door. Old Bruce's breakfast maneuver and the known dimensions of the jail building allow a guess that "le chaine" was at least eight feet long. This assumes it was fastened to the wall opposite the door, and that Chambreau, shackled perhaps by an ankle, could stretch out about seven feet from ankle to fingertips.

The use of the chain would seem to confirm the impression that the jail per se wasn't very secure. In fact, British law by the 1840s made chaining illegal unless there was danger of escape.[31]

It seems significant that Chambreau, writing his memoir in English, used the French term "le chaine" to refer to the jail's shackle. Evidently the chain was such a well-known feature that he could assume his readers would know what he meant.

One of the benefits of being tended by the kitchen staff, apparently, was getting regular meals. Chambreau's reference to "breakfast" implies there were other meals which would indicate that the Fort's jailbirds were better fed than the law required. British law said only that prisoners had to receive a daily ration of bread and water.

How often the Fort Vancouver jail had tenants is unclear. But now and then the Fort's records mention them.

Among the first to be incarcerated were two Hawaiians who broke into a storeroom in September 1844 and got drunk on rum while their co-workers fought an advancing forest fire. They were flogged at the gun on Oct. 1, and jailed for an unknown term. Three other men who had fled the fire in a panic were placed in irons and "taken out (into the yard, apparently) and exposed to the contempt and derision of all their fellow servants," McLoughlin noted in a report.[32]

On Aug. 19, 1845, a French-Canadian who tried to desert was given 13 lashes and "put in prison." He stayed there until Aug. 30 when two friends put up a £20 bond to guarantee that he wouldn't run away again.[33]

3. NOTES

1. Besides problems of custom, there was a language barrier. Harvey, op. cit., p. 20, mentions an unusual case in which insurrectionist Ambroise Lepine was tried in a mixed court shortly after modern Canada united in 1870. This awkward proceeding dragged tediously in dual translation. At one point, a defense lawyer named Royal addressed the jury alternately in English and French for close to eight hours.

2. 40 George III chapter 138.

3. McLoughlin's letters, 1st series, op. cit., pp. xxxix ff.

4. 40 George III chapter 138.

5. See generally Harvey, op. cit.

6. 1&2 George IV chapter 66.

7. E.E. Rich. *History of the Hudson's Bay Company*. Hudson's Bay Record Society, London 1959, II, pp. 401-05.

8. 1&2 George IV chapter 66.

9. Ibid.

10. Neither the statute itself nor a cursory examination of English criminal enactments around that time gives a clue as to why parliament chose a cutoff date of Sept. 17, 1792 for the laws it transferred to Canada.

11. "Egyptians" meant gypsies. They were heavily persecuted in England, branded as vagabonds and thieves. 5 Elizabeth chapter 20, adopted 1593, made it a felony without benefit of clergy to keep steady company with gypsies. This absurdity was still on the books when the English criminal code was grafted onto Ontario in 1800, thereby becoming applicable in Oregon, at least in theory, with the first Fur Trade Act in 1803.

12. The capriciousness of 19th Century English death penalty laws was lamented by many authorities including the pre-eminent legal scholar and judge, Sir William Blackstone. One of the most readable and scholarly books on English criminal law is Blackstone's *Commentaries on the Laws of*

England (Rees Welsh, Philadelphia 1902). See particularly pp. 4-5. Also, Leon Radzinowicz, *History of English Criminal Law* (Stevens & Sons, London 1848), I, 450-71.

13. 40 George III chapter 1, "An Act for the further introduction of the Criminal Law of England in this province, and for the more effectual Punishment of certain Offenders," enacted July 4, 1800. Published in *The Statutes of His Majesty's Province of Upper Canada, 1818 edition.*

14. Ibid.

15. Ibid.

16. Harvey, p. 13.

17. Harvey, pp. 13-14.

18. Details are murky but only one employee was actually named as the shooter, Urbain Heroux, who claimed he was protecting himself.

19. Rich's introduction to McLoughlin's 1839-44 letters, pp. xliv-ix, gives a concise account of the dispute over the younger McLoughlin death.

20. Ibid.

21. George IV chapter 31, enacted June 27, 1828, extensively revised the English criminal code. Section 7 of the statute allowed British subjects to be prosecuted in England even for offenses committed on foreign soil. Thom apparently wasn't aware that similar authority had been given to Canadian courts in the original 1803 fur trade statute, 40 George III, Chapter 138. This law, which was clarified but not superceded by the 1821 statute, said "subjects of his Majesty shall be tried [for crimes under Canadian laws] although offence be committed in another European state."

22. Cited by Rich in his introduction to McLoughlin's letters, 2nd series, above.

23. John A. Hussey. *Fort Vancouver Historic Structures Report.* National Park Service, 1972, p. 438.

24. Hussey, p. 445.

25. Chambreau, p. 10, above.

26. See Jessett, p. 86, above. A biographical sketch of William Bruce appears in Hudson's Bay Miscellaney, p. 309, above.

27. Ibid. Also see *McLoughlin's Fort Vancouver Letters*, 2nd series, letter of June 26, 1844. Also see John Warren Dease, *Memorandum Book*, 1829, MS, entry for Oct. 15, 1829, cited by Hussey, p. 172.

28. George Roberts. "The Round Hand of George B. Roberts." *Oregon Historical Quarterly*, vol. 63, 1962, p. 225. Also see Hussey, Historic Structures Report Historic Data Volume 1. National Park Service, 1972, pp. 170-72.

29. McLoughlin letter to governor and committee, cited by Hussey manuscript p. 440.

30. Hussey manuscript, p. 447.

31. A catalogue of 18th Century English prison abuses was compiled by John Howard in *The State of Prisons in England and Wales* (Warrington, London 1784). The practice of extorting money from convicts by offering them their choice of irons, or removing them altogether, is described on pages 13-14.

32. McLoughlin's letters, 2nd series, p. 44.

33. Hussey manuscript, p. 440.

4.
"...vicious immoral or indolent habits..."

Several years before McLoughlin built his jailhouse, emphasizing his governmental authority, the handful of Americans south of the Columbia River began talking about forming a government of their own. One subject they debated was whether to adopt criminal laws.

It was a controversial issue because crime was almost non-existent in Oregon. The handful of American residents included a high proportion of Protestant missionaries and their assistants, few of whom seemed likely to turn bandit. Some people argued that adopting a code would just give outsiders a bad impression of their community. It was a vestige of the early-American belief that a virtuous community was created naturally by virtuous citizens, and that anti-crime laws, however severe, could never produce the same result.

Among those who agreed with this position was Commodore Charles Wilkes, a distinguished U.S. Navy oceanographer and explorer who visited the Oregon settlement in 1841. Wilkes told the American leaders that "any laws they might establish would be a poor substitute for the moral code they all now followed, and that evil-doers would not be disposed to settle near a community entirely opposed to their practices."

Wilkes believed that criminal laws would only "advertise the community's lack of moral force to control itself and prevent crime."[1]

Odd as it may sound, the idea that a community could rule itself best with "moral force" and the habit of civic virtue was not a radical idea in 1841. The majority of the Americans who heard Wilkes' views must have agreed with him because they didn't pass the proposed laws.

Most of the Oregon leaders who took part in the discussions had grown up in American communities that governed themselves in the manner Wilkes favored. Laws and officials in that era were at a minimum, and communities were ruled much in the manner of an extended family.

For most of America in 1841, government was still uncomplicated and very much a local affair. Relatively few laws were as yet on the books, and there weren't many officials to enforce them. Not even the largest American city had a full-time police department until Philadelphia established one in 1833. Another two decades went by until uniforms were introduced. It wasn't until 1856 that New York City became the first city with a uniformed police force.[2]

Passing elaborate criminal laws, building penitentiaries, and hiring full-time police to see that people refrained from misbehavior would have struck earlier Americans as weird.

In his classic social study, *The Discovery of the Asylum*, David J. Rothman points out that order in a typical early American town was maintained not by "law enforcement" but by the natural social bonds of the community. Not only did the inhabitants of small American towns know one another well, but were often related by blood or marriage, and usually attended the same church. Social relationships were not haphazard. People understood what was expected of them and their neighbors. They dwelt within a hierarchy that placed God at the top, followed by persons who were thought to be familiar with God's will—the community's wealthy people and the clergy.

Although town leaders were entitled to obedience and respect, the benefits of hierarchy had to flow down as well as up. Wealthier people were under Divine obligation to see to the needs of less fortunate neighbors. Widows and orphans had to be looked after.

Because there was no federal or state government to fall back on, communities had to be careful about taking in newcomers who might drain the town's alms or cause trouble. People who arrived without a letter of reference from their former church, or who lacked an evident means of self-support, as in the case of widows with young children, were apt to be "warned out" of town by the local Overseers of the Poor.

Interestingly, two "Overseers of the Poor" were in the list of officials that Oregon settlers proposed for their provisional government in 1841.[3]

The kinds of social controls that early Americans used in lieu of law-enforcement reflected not only the era's simplicity but also a different set of assumptions about human behavior. They didn't regard crime as something to be expected in a society, any more than a family would regard crime within the family as normal. Moreover, social pressure within communities encouraged positively virtuous conduct.

Public safety didn't just require suppressing crime. It required cooperation among community members, and required honorable conduct. In other words, people had to adhere strictly to the social contract. Their survival depended on it, not just their peace of mind. With survival at stake, small town early-Americans took a keen interest in whether their neighbors were industrious or lazy, drunk or sober, church-going or impious. People didn't draw a fine distinction between "crime" and "sin."

If someone broke the social contract, how it was broken wasn't as important as the fact that it was broken. A matter that might be considered private today—adultery for instance—was of public concern in early America, not just because it offended religious sensibilities, but because it could affect the peace and unity of the group. The same was true of other "private" offenses, such as drunkenness, idleness, or breaking the Sabbath.

Punishments for those types of transgressions were usually not severe in physical terms, but psychologically they were often excruciating. Drunks, idlers or minor thieves, so labeled, suffered a severe loss of status that was difficult if not impossible to live down. Offenders might be shunned socially or made to suffer public humiliation such as being put in the stocks on the town square. Those who repeated their offense or committed a really serious crime such as housebreaking or blasphemy could be expelled from the town or even hanged.

But as Rothman points out, early-day Americans would have thought it odd indeed had anyone suggested putting wrongdoers in a penitentiary for an extended period of time to try to discover the cause of their wrongdoing and "cure" them.[4]

Early Americans did not have to inquire into the cause of wrongdoing because they already knew the cause: People were born in a state of Original Sin[5] and therefore were inclined by nature to commit evil. The fact that people did sometimes commit evil came as no surprise.

The connection between the moral behavior of individuals and the peaceful prosperity of society as a whole was taken as self-evident by the directors of the Hudson's Bay Company. Religious books were furnished to Fort Vancouver residents at Company expense. Sunday church attendance was compulsory. The board advised McLoughlin that Divine services were to be "publickly read with becoming solemnity for every man woman and child" and for all Indians "whom it will be proper to invite."

McLoughlin was instructed to "see that in the course of the week, all irregularity, vicious immoral or indolent habits are checked and discountenanced and their opposites encouraged and rewarded."[6]

The interests of God, England and the Hudson's Bay Company were seen as interlocked. When the Company sent Rev. Beaver to be Fort Vancouver's chaplain, it gave him an elaborate silver communion service engraved with the Company coat-of-arms.[7]

The board's edict that McLoughlin invite Indians to church was as much for home consumption as for the welfare of Indians. Their treatment at the hands of the Company was a particularly sensitive political subject in England, which was sprouting reform movements of all sorts.

But not everything the Company did to mollify its critics was flim-flam. Indians actually were invited to services at the Fort, and as a practical matter the Company did try to get along with indigenous peoples because the fur trade required it. McLoughlin assured London that his men were reminded regularly that "wanton murder of Indians exposed them to capital indictments in Canada."[8]

But there was no such thing as treating Indians as equals. And, for that matter, the Indians preferred not to treat Company people as equals whenever they could do otherwise. The Company treated its non-British laborers and its Indians somewhat alike, which is to say like useful livestock.

The Americans in Oregon tended to vacillate in their relationships with the Indians between idealistic folly and whatever its opposite was. Settlers thought they could get along just fine without laws, but they didn't think Indians could.

Dr. Elijah White, a former missionary leader who somehow got himself appointed federal Indian sub-agent for Oregon, drew up a code of laws for the Nez Perce to follow that included elaborate penalties for violations, including floggings, fines and hangings.

The laws were to be enforced by a new form of Nez Perce government that White dreamed up that was entirely alien to tribal custom. They were supposed to choose a principal chief who would act as a sort of governor, with 12 subordinate chiefs as a cabinet or privy council.

The laws were as follows:

Article 1. Whoever willfully take life shall be hung.

Article 2. Whoever burns a dwelling house shall be hung.

Article 3. Whoever burns an out-building shall be imprisoned six months, receive 50 lashes and pay all damages.

Article 4. Whoever carelessly burns a house, or any property, shall pay damages.

Article 5. If anyone enter a dwelling, without permission of the occupant, the chiefs shall punish him as they think proper. Public rooms are excepted.

Article 6. If anyone steal he shall pay back twofold; and if it be the value of a beaver skin or less, he shall receive 25 lashes; and if the value is over a beaver skin he shall pay back twofold, and receive 50 lashes.

Article 7. If anyone take a horse and ride it, without permission, or take any article and use it, without liberty, he shall pay for the use of it, and receive from 20 to 50 lashes as the chief shall direct.

Article 8. If anyone enter a field, and injure the crops, or throw down the fence, so that cattle or horses go in and do damage, he shall pay all damages, and receive 25 lashes for every offense.

Article 9. Those only may keep dogs who travel or live among the game; if a dog kill a lamb, calf, or any domestic animal, the owner shall pay the damages and kill the dog.

Article 10. If an Indian raise a gun or other weapon against a white man, it shall be reported to the chiefs, and they shall punish it. If a white does the same to an Indian, it shall be reported to Dr. White, and he shall punish or redress it.

Article 11. If an Indian break these laws, he shall be punished by his chiefs; if a white man break them, he shall be reported to the agent and punished at his instance.[9]

The laws, in other words, made a lot of promises that couldn't be kept. Fiasco ensued.

"The Indians," one observer reported, "wanted pay for being whipped in compliance with Dr. White's laws, the same as they did for praying to please the missionaries during the great Indian revival of 1839."

When White refused to give the Nez Perce pants and blankets as a reward for accepting his laws, they revolted. They threw away the laws and discarded the flogging tools, seeing no benefit from this strange custom of the white man. They explained that they "had been whipped a good many times and had got nothing for it, and it had done them no good."[10]

McLoughlin never did anything as absurd as White did, but he got in trouble anyway for going too far accepting Indian custom. Beaver, after his final rift with McLoughlin, returned to England and tried to get him fired for allowing Indian slaves to be kept at Fort Vancouver, among other misdeeds.

The Aborigines Protection Society of London published a muckraking article by Beaver charging that 80 to 90 Indians were "owned by persons of all classes in the Company's service, and by those who have retired from it, and become settlers on the rivers Willamette and Cowlitz, but over whom the Company retain authority."

Beaver declared in his piece that, "I knew some of (the Indian slaves) to be flogged by order of the officer in charge of the establishment, others to be cruelly ill-used by their owners. The women themselves, who were living with the lower class of the Company's servants, were much in the condition of slaves, being purchased by their Indian proprietors or relations, and not infrequently re-sold amongst each other by their purchasers."[11]

William A. Slacum, an American spy who toured Oregon in the 1830s, charged that the Fort's officers encouraged employees to own Indian slaves because it increased the labor supply without increasing payroll expenses.[12]

But whom exactly was to blame and to what degree wasn't that clear. Long before the Hudson's Bay Company arrived in the Northwest, local Indians had regularly enslaved each other, encouraging the arriving fur traders to take up their bad habit—one that McLoughlin didn't disallow. An argument could be made that it wasn't a case of the Company debauching the Indians but the Indians debauching the Company.[13]

The unenviable status of Indian slaves was noted in an 1832 incident in which one was slain, along with a Company cow, by Cayuse tribesmen near Fort Walla Walla. McLoughlin wrote to his Walla Walla manager, Simon McGillivray, advising him not to overreact.

McLoughlin wrote:

You know that altho' the killing of Sasty is murder yet with these Indians it is considered no greater offence than killing a horse; and perhaps not so bad as the shooting of the cow. God forbid that I should mean to justify Murder, but in dealing with the Indians we ought to make allowance for their manner of thinking and if I was addressed on the subject by any of them I would say the Almighty has forbid the shedding of innocent blood, and commanded that he who shed man's blood by man shall his blood be shed. And in obedience to this command, if a Chief among us was to Kill a slave that Chief would be killed. But as you have not the means of putting this command in execution you will leave it to the Almighty who will punish the Murderer either in this world or the world to come.

McLoughlin also had some managerial misgivings that made him wary of trying to confront the murderers. Writing to another official, McLoughlin said: "It appears to me injudicious in us to neglect our business to send a party to punish an Indian who may go out of our reach and if the Tribe are willing to defend him can put us to defiance - But even if we did Kill him, it might be the cause of deranging all our business along the [Columbia River]."[14]

When circumstances permitted, the Company did move against refractory Indians, sometimes indiscriminately. According to Beaver, Hudson's Bay employees slaughtered Native Americans at least three times on the Oregon Coast for interfering with Company business. Beaver said he was "reliably informed" that two of the reprisal raids in 1835-36 claimed about a dozen Native lives, and that the raiders in one case burned a village, and "threw a child into a fire" to avenge the alleged theft of some horses and a knife.[15]

McLoughlin in April 1832 sent a feared lieutenant, Michel LaFramboise, to raid a Tillamook village following the murder in that vicinity of two company trappers, Pierre Kakaraquiron and Thomas Canasawarette, both of whom were partly of Native descent.

"I shall not shackle you with copious instructions," McLoughlin jotted to LaFramboise. "Permit me, however, to recommend that as 'tis likely some innocent beings may in such cases unavoidably become victims as well as the guilty the severity necessary, for our own safety & security may always be tempered with humanity and mercy."[16]

McLoughlin was much relieved, later on, to hear that his raiders had killed "only" six members of the offending tribe, not all of whom, incidentally, were clearly implicated in the murders. McLoughlin instructed LaFramboise to get word to the survivors that the Company expected them to "Kill the remainder of the murderers of our people— if they do not we will return and will not spare one of the tribe."[17]

Although the sanctioned killing of Indians was a normal if infrequent part of Company procedure, private individuals were discouraged from taking matters into their own hands.

In a July 2, 1830 letter to an associate, McLoughlin expressed annoyance at a report that one of his employees, William Kittson, had offered a bounty of two horses for the murder of a certain Indian. "Will you have the Goodness to state to Mr. Kittson," McLoughlin fumed, "that the Company will not allow such proceedings and that it must not be done—It is only when Indians have murdered any of the Company Servants (employees) or any person belonging to the Establishment that we can have a Right to Kill the Murderer or get him Killed."[18]

However, McLoughlin defended one of his clerks, Francis Ermatinger, for sending an Indian interpreter named Lolo to cut off the earlobe of another Indian who had stolen Ermatinger's woman. McLoughlin explained to headquarters that "if the Indian had not been punished it would have lowered the Whites in their Estimation as among themselves they never allow such an offence to pass unpunished."[19]

Black Douglas, McLoughlin's redoubtable second-in-command, helped beat an Indian to death at Stuart Lake, Alaska, in 1828 after recognizing him as someone who had committed a murder several years earlier at Fort George. After killing the suspect, Douglas had his body dragged to a public place to be eaten by dogs.[20]

Hardly any gentler was Douglas's treatment of a Native chief who had murdered a Company servant at Fort Vancouver. In a gesture of contempt, the chief returned boldly to his encampment near the Fort, boasting that nothing could be done to him because his tribe was too powerful. Douglas took a gun, walked through the Indian camp to the chief's lodge and went in and shot him dead in the midst of his astonished companions.[21]

Other reprisals were conducted more decorously, giving at least a pretense of legality.

The earliest quasi-legal execution in Oregon for which there is any record took place at Fort George—Astoria—in the fall of 1814. Several Indians had murdered a blacksmith and two other employees of the North West Company as they made charcoal in a nearby woods. The presumably guilty parties were arrested with the help of Chief Concomly and taken back to the fort to be dealt with.

"The prisoners were confined in the bastion, and next morning led out, blindfolded, to be shot," reported Peter Corney, a witness.

> They were placed opposite a 6-pounder (cannon), while a party of rifle-men were in the bastion ready to fire through the loop-holes, which manouevre was made use of in order to make the Indians believe that they were shot by the great gun. The dead bodies were taken down to the wharf in coffins, and exposed for some days, till their friends were allowed to carry them away.[22]

Corney didn't say how many Indians were executed or what sort of hearing, if any, preceded it.

The record is a little better in the case of McLoughlin's disposal of an Indian accused of murdering two Hudson's Bay employees near Fort George in August 1840. John McKay, a half-Indian, and an unidentified Indian boy, were shot in their sleep after they'd spent the day salting salmon near Pillar Rock on the Columbia River.

A Company reprisal party gunned down two Indian suspects and brought a third back to Fort George for an "examination," as one report put it. The Rev. John H. Frost, a Methodist missionary working in the area, noted in his diary that the captured Quinault hadn't committed the murders himself but was thought to have been "as deeply implicated as the slave (who supposedly had fired the murder weapon.)"[23]

McLoughlin arrived at Fort George August 29 and took charge of the proceedings, assisted by a Company physician, Dr. William F.

Tolmie, and an American sea captain, John H. Couch, who had just arrived in Astoria on the brig Maryland.[24]

This three-party court resembled superficially the sort of tribunal that the 1821 Fur Trade Act permitted. However, it couldn't have been legally constituted because this would have required an order from the Queen's Bench of Upper Canada. Also, McLoughlin couldn't have claimed to act under the war powers clause of the Company charter, because the charter applied only to Rupert's Land. Fort George was as far outside Rupert's Land as it was possible to go without falling into the Pacific Ocean.

In short, McLoughlin dressed up a bit of ritual to resemble a court, and he probably made a creditable judge with his long silver hair, steely blue eyes and grave manner. Unfortunately for the Quinault there was no appeal from McLoughlin's sentence. The Indian, Frost wrote, "was adjudged worthy of death according to the laws of Great Britain and America. He was therefore, by order of the Governor (McLoughlin), hung by the neck until he was dead at 1 o'clock p.m."[25]

In truth, it was more of a public strangulation than a hanging. A long rope was thrown over a scaffold and McLoughlin and the 30 or 40 men in attendance took the end of it and yanked the condemned man off his feet.

Of the non-Indians present, only the Rev. Frost declined to take part, although he refused to criticize those who did.[26]

It is necessary for the safety of the community that the (Indians) be punished," Frost wrote. "It is very evident that the reason why any farther depredations are not committed, is not because they love the whites, but because they fear punishment. There are no doubt a few exceptions.[27]

The Astoria case wasn't the first in which a do-it-yourself tribunal was convened in a homicide case.

Three members of Oregon's tiny American community had held an inquest five years earlier into a love-triangle killing on Wapato —now Sauvie—Island. Thomas Jefferson Hubbard, a gunsmith, had shot and killed a drunken tailor named Thornburg who tried to crawl through the window of his cabin during the early hours of July 4, 1835.

According to testimony, the two men were rivals for the affections of a woman who had jilted Thornburg and moved in with Hubbard. Thornburg was well-snockered, as usual, when he armed himself with a knife and gun and tried to reclaim her. Hubbard told the tribunal he shot Thornburg twice and battled him hand-to-hand until he expired.

John Kirk Townsend, a visiting naturalist who participated in the inquest, was able to put things in perspective for his two fellow panelists, based on personal experience. Townsend said he once hired Thornburg to carry scientific specimens he collected on a field trip through Oregon and that Thornburg, whose habits he was unaware of, decanted a jug of rare lizards and snakes and got drunk on the preservative alcohol, dealing science a severe blow.[28]

The other panel members, James L. Lambert, a visiting ship's captain, and Courtney M. Walker, an American trader, agreed after hearing the snakes-and-lizards testimony, that Thornburg's death was "justifiable homicide." They gave Hubbard a sworn account of the proceedings "to prevent difficulty, if the subject should ever be investigated in the future," Townsend said.[29]

There were some other early efforts at formalized justice in Oregon's American community.

In 1838, three years after the Thornburg case, David M. Leslie was appointed by other members of the Methodist Mission to act as "justice of the peace." The appointment had no apparent legal basis, but nobody seems to have objected.

Leslie's entire judicial career consisted of trying an Indian woman for theft.

The outcome was not recorded.[30]

4. NOTES

1. Edmond S. Meany, ed. "Diary of Wilkes in the Northwest." *Washington Historical Quarterly*, vol. 16, pp. 48-9.

2. Harry Elmer Barnes and Negley K. Teeters. *New Horizons in Criminology*, 3rd ed. Prentice Hall, 1960, p. 213.

3. *The Oregon Archives*, ed. La Fayette Grover. Asahel Bush, Public Printer, Salem OR 1853, p. 5.

4. David J. Rothman. *The Discovery of the Asylum*. Little, Brown, NY 1971.

5. In orthodox Christian belief, the parents of the human race committed "Original Sin" with all its consequences for future generations by disobeying God in the Garden of Eden. Besides being expelled from Eden, Adam and Eve suffered a darkening of intellect and a weakening of will, which was inclined tragically toward evil. The new condition of the human race became one of continual moral struggle and dependence on God. Although the doctrine of Original Sin was, upon analysis, profoundly optimistic, it did not view people in their natural state as the enormously perfectible beings imagined by the philosophers of the Enlightenment. It was the latter set of ideas that lay behind the first penitentiaries.

6. Compulsory church attendance, although seldom rigorously enforced, wasn't an unusual rule in British colonies. The Company's Sunday piety requirement is recounted in *Minutes of Council of Northern Department of Rupert's Land*, p. 174, above.

7. John A. Hussey, *The History of Fort Vancouver and its Physical Structure*. Washington State Historical Society, Tacoma WA 1957, p. 174.

8. McLoughlin's letters, 2nd series, p. 117.

9. Gray, p. 228, above.

10. Gustavus Hines' report cited by Gray, pp. 310-11.

11. Beaver's letter to the Aborigines Protection Society, cited by Pipes, p. 336.

12. Document: "Slacum's Report on Oregon, 1836-37," *Oregon Historical Quarterly*, vol. 13, 1912, p. 192.

13. See Elsie Frances Dennis, "Indian Slavery in Pacific Northwest," (three parts), *Oregon Historical Quarterly*, vol. 31, 1930, pp. 69-81, 181-95 and 285-96.

14. McLoughlin's letters, 1st series, p. 258.

15. Beaver's letter to the Aborigines Protection Society, p. 338, above.

16. *Letters of Dr. John McLoughlin*, ed. Burt B. Barker. Binfords & Mort, Portland OR 1948, p. 268.

17. McLoughlin letter quoted by Barker, p. 272, above.

18. McLoughlin letter quoted by Barker, p. 109, above. Although the charter's war clause didn't allow individuals to kill Indians for private purposes, McLoughlin's correspondence indicates that the Company did sanction hiring Indians to kill other Indians under certain circumstances. Also see McLoughlin's letters, 1st series, p. 57.

19. McLoughlin's letters, first series, p. 185, above.

20. *Servant of Two Empires*. Derek Pethek, James Douglas. Mitchell Press, Vancouver 1969, p. 17.

21. Gustavus Hines, *Oregon: Its History, Condition and Prospects*. Geo. H. Derby & Co., Buffalo NY 1851, p. 392.

22. Cited by J. Neilson Barry in "Peter Corney's Voyages, 1814-17," *Oregon Historical Quarterly*, vol. 33, pp. 361-62

23. "Journal of John H. Frost," ed. Nellie B. Pipes, *Oregon Historical Quarterly*, vol. 35, 1934, p. 61.

24. Daniel Lee and Joseph H. Frost. *Ten Years In Oregon*. Arno Press, NY 1973, p. 270 ff.

25. Ibid.

26. Hines, p. 391, above.

27. Frost's Journal, p. 60, above.

28. John Kirk Townsend. *Narrative of a Journey*. Ye Galleon Press, Fairfield WA 1970, p. 325. Also see Oswald West, "First White Settlers on French Prairie," *Oregon Historical Quarterly*, vol. 43, p. 204.

29. Townsend, p. 234, above.

30. Lee and Frost, p. 274. Gray says in his *History of Oregon*, p. 198, that Leslie presided as judge in the Hubbard case. John Kirk Townsend wrote an account of his own participation, naming himself and two other men as the jurors. Curiously, he didn't mention Leslie. It could have been an oversight, but it's also possible that Gray was mistaken in placing Leslie there. Leslie's ad hoc "appointment" as a justice of the peace didn't occur until three years later.

5.
Immigrants, bureaucrats and lash laws

As the 1840s began, there was still no American law in Oregon. There was some semblance of British law, but its reach was uncertain, leaving Oregon in the political and legal limbo created in 1818 by the U.S.-British joint-occupancy treaty.

The U.S. wanted its boundary with Canada to follow the 49th parallel straight west from Ontario to the Pacific Ocean. Britain accepted the line only as far as the upper Columbia River, insisting that it follow the river from that point to the ocean and thus give Canada present-day Washington state and, importantly for British maritime interests, Puget Sound.[1]

It was by no means clear that the American position would prevail.

The U.S. government's interest in Oregon was so slight that Secretary of State Daniel Webster tried to use it as a diplomatic bargaining chip. In 1842, he offered to accept Britain's position on the boundary if Britain would help the U.S. take California from Mexico.[2]

Oregon was still a power-politics piñata with an uncertain future as the Nineteenth Century entered its fourth decade. This had potentially serious consequences for the approximately 250 Americans and 700 or so British subjects living there. Lack of a sovereign government left them with no sure way to handle important problems such as getting secure title to land they claimed and establishing law-and-order.

Many in this mixed community wanted to create a stopgap government on their own authority. But how would this happen? Who would be able to get everybody together to do it?

A dead man, it turned out.

Ewing Young, a wealthy entrepreneur who'd made a lot of his money running a whiskey still, died suddenly and without heirs on Feb. 9, 1841, leaving a sizable estate.[3] Nearly everybody who was anybody attended Young's funeral and the main topic was how to get their hands on the old boy's money.

Young not only had left a considerable pile of cash but an apparently valid claim to a whole valley of prime farmland and a herd of horses that McLoughlin suspected him of stealing. Whose property was it now?

Normally an heirless estate passed to the government, but Oregon as yet had no government. The settlers agreed it was high time to form one.

On Feb. 17, with Young barely planted, several dozen settlers assembled at a farmhouse at Champoeg, southwest of Oregon City, and voted to create a provisional government to take Young's estate. They elected a "Constitutional Committee" and chose Ira Babcock, a 33-year-old New York doctor and member of the Methodist Mission, as "Supreme Judge" who would also act as governor. William Johnson, a 56-year-old former British sailor, was picked as High Sheriff. Three constables were appointed to assist him, but it's unclear what Johnson did, if anything, as High Sheriff. He and his wife, Polly, a member of the Chehalis tribe, and their two children, lived in an isolated cabin in what is now downtown Portland.

Although records are sparse, it can be said with certainty that Johnson was Oregon's first official law enforcement officer. And he was a notable character as well. He'd quit the Royal Navy to serve on the American side in the War of 1812. As a crewman on the USS Constitution—Old Ironsides—he received a blow to the head by a British saber that left a big scar that he wore as a badge of honor.

Making his way to the Pacific Northwest in the 1820s he became a fur trapper and mountain man. He joined a Hudson's Bay expedition to explore the Fraser River and Puget Sound where he met Polly, the love of his life. He brought her down to Oregon where they settled in the French-Canadian colony at Champoeg. He became a farmer, and in 1841 he and Polly hosted Commodore Wilkes, the U.S. Navy oceanographer, at their farmhouse. They shared with him their extensive knowledge of the region to help Wilkes write a report for the President.[4]

Immigrants arriving in the Willamette Valley in 1842 brought news that thrilled and alarmed the people already living there. Oregon fever was sweeping the East and a land-rush was imminent. Hundreds and possibly thousands of newcomers would soon be rolling into Oregon with visions of free land dancing in their heads.

It was a wake-up call for the stakeholder residents who couldn't be sure their land claims would withstand any challenges.

Only a real government could issue legal title to a piece of property, and the older residents could only show documents they'd more or less issued to themselves. They didn't know what might happen if a stranger showed up who might try to claim the same property.

Land titles had been uppermost in their minds since 1840, at least, when citizens sent Congress a petition asking that Oregon be made part of the United States. It was a shrewd political document because it didn't harp on real estate, which might have made them sound greedy, but emphasized that they were American citizens and entitled to the protection of the American government. As things stood, they said, the colony could only muster "self-constituted tribunals originated and sustained by the power of an ill-constructed public opinion and the resort to force of arms."[5]

To repeat a familiar refrain, the thing uppermost in residents' minds was not a sheriff to protect them from killers or outlaws or an army to ward off Indian attacks, but a government that could issue land titles. In other words, they wanted clerks. Government clerks. County clerks especially.

A mere county clerk with a well-inked pad and a rubber stamp could turn a land claim into a legal deed of ownership with one whack.

A clerk would know how to handle the paperwork, where to put the notary seal and how to record the deed in the County Book of Deeds. Once recorded, the deed would be proof positive of the owner's right to the described property, per omnia saecula saeculorum.

Clerks and bureaucrats would be as essential to peacekeeping on the Oregon frontier as any sheriff, jailer or penitentiary superintendent.

But before clerks could be appointed, another question would have to be answered first: What sovereign government would appoint them?

As the 1840s began, there was no certain answer.

The U.S.-British Treaty of Joint Occupation was still in force and it was yet to be decided which country would end up with Oregon.

This further complicated the question of land claims. American settlers feared their claims might not recognized if Oregon became a possession of Great Britain. The same was true, in reverse, for Oregon's British residents—mostly retirees of the Hudson's Bay Company. Many had lived in Oregon since the 1820s and were afraid that an American government might dispossess them.

Uncertainty about land ownership rights was a significant source of conflict among settlers of all sorts and especially the Americans.

"One can hardly leave his place for a moment without having his claim jumped," wrote John Todd, a Fort Vancouver clerk. "The practice has already led to several boxing matches amongst these worthies, and it is to be apprehended may result in acts more fatal ere long."[6]

Whether a claim had been jumped, or not jumped, could be open to dispute without an official and exact description of what was being claimed and when. So, without clerks, recorders or survey maps, a claim was just that, and barely worth the paper it was written on.

Mapmaking was serious business and there was no one to do it. Marking a property by the location of a tree or rock or a meandering stream or other natural feature was less than satisfactory since trees could be cut down, rocks moved or some other feature altered accidentally or on purpose. Exactness required official surveys and survey maps, which required a public surveyor who could not exist without a government.

A sheriff could evict trespassers or even arrest them, but first there had to be proof that trespassers were trespassing. Without it, the sheriff was relegated to dealing with murderers and robbers who were far less numerous in pioneer Oregon than claim-jumpers.

Civil courts, another institution requiring a government, also helped keep the peace by giving people a means to settle disputes, including those over property, without violence.

As long as land was plentiful, violent confrontations were infrequent. But yearly immigration brought more people into Oregon and created more chances of conflict. Which is why the services of a real government with real bureaucrats were sorely missed.

In May 1843, as a wagon train with a record 900 immigrants headed west from Missouri, a second community meeting was convened in Champoeg to rejuvenate the Provisional government.

The vote this time was a squeaker—52 in favor to 50 opposed. Most of the "No" votes were cast by former Hudson's Bay employees wary of American control.

On July 5, the Americans set up their new government. They created a three-member executive committee to act as governor, a nine-member legislative committee to pass laws, and a judiciary. Then they elected officers to fill all the posts.

Alanson Beers, a Methodist Mission member and future business partner of Mission Chief Steward George Abernethy, was seated on both the Executive and Legislative committees of the Provisional government, assuring that satisfactory laws were passed.

The Mission over time had become largely a business, competing with other businesses including the Hudson's Bay Company and some personal enterprises of John McLoughlin.

The Organic Laws adopted by the Provisional government were based on the laws of the Iowa Territory, with a few new wrinkles added that benefitted the Mission. While settlers were limited to land claims of as little as 320 acres, "missions of a religious character" were allowed 3,840 acres.

The new laws also took aim at McLoughlin's mills and warehouses at Willamette Falls.

"No person," the Provisional government decided, "shall be entitled to hold...extensive water privileges or other situations necessary for the transaction of Mercantile or Manufacturing operations and to the detriment of the community."

This put McLoughlin in a serious bind, but he was about to win potential allies: the new settlers rolling into Oregon.

"We were kindly treated by Dr. McLoughlin," wagon boss James Nesmith wrote in his diary concerning a stopover at Fort Vancouver. McLoughlin, he said, "gave us a good dinner and showed us other courtesies."

When the 1843 party reached the Willamette Valley and organized a new government, they threw out the land laws favoring the Methodist Mission and addressed others that put them at a disadvantage. The rules governing land claim rules were at the head of the list.

Single men found they could claim only half as much land as they'd expected—320 acres instead of the full 640 available to married men. There were lots of single men in the 1843 party, especially single young men, so those who wanted to get 640 acres needed a bride.

But that was a bit of a problem. Marriageable young women were as scarce on the Oregon frontier as horse feathers.

So, the new government did the only thing it could do: expand the supply of eligible females.

How? Simply by reducing the legal age for girls to marry to 14.

This wouldn't have shocked many people in the 1840s. Early marriage was common in America at that time. No less a personage than John Marshal, chief justice of the U.S. Supreme Court, married a 14-year-old girl and there was no public comment.

In fact, many states followed British common law allowing girls to marry at 12. For boys it was 14.

Letting early-adolescent girls marry probably did as much to keep the peace in Oregon at this particular time as any gun-toting sheriff. With better opportunity to marry, single men with real estate on their mind and not sex, necessarily, were less likely to get into fights over the few adult single women west of St. Louis. Or to court disaster by making a play for somebody else's wife.

The 1843 migration also wrought change in the political climate.

The newcomers arrived in Oregon not just with their plows and dishes and kitchen tables, but also their social mores.

Most opposed slavery. They did so on moral grounds or because they wanted to avoid the strife that was starting to tear the rest of the country apart. Or both. Or for any number of other reasons.

The historian Frances Fuller Victor put the slavery question to old-time pioneer Joe Meek in an interview at his home in Hillsboro in 1875. She was interested in the seeming contradiction between the immigrants' opposition to slavery and their embrace of anti-Black laws. The answer was complicated.

Most of the new homesteaders were from border states where slavery persisted to a certain degree, and also from southern states where it was legal. But not every southern or border-state was pro-slavery, Meek pointed out, not because they were racially sensitive, necessarily, but because different classes of people saw life differently. Only a minority of whites owned slaves, and this created a two-tiered social structure that put wealthy slave-owning whites at the top and people who owned no slaves and did their own labor feeling poor and looked down-upon.

"Perhaps having experienced the disadvantages of being 'poor whites' in a slave-holding community, and being without the means of procuring slaves, they (the new immigrants) resolved to prevent any future influx of slave-holders, who should reduce them to the condition of 'poor whites' in the country of their adoption," Victor summed up.[7]

Although the evidence shows that a majority of the settlers opposed slavery, that didn't mean they wanted free Black neighbors, either. Just about every state in the Union had Black Exclusion laws that discouraged free Blacks from taking up residence. The laws worked by imposing all sorts of rules and restrictions that made their lives miserable. Blacks were depicted as an inferior species and as troublemakers, and as a potential drain on community resources.

Missouri, home state of most of Oregon's 1843 immigrants, had a typical Black law that said any free Black found within the state could be ordered to leave. It was illegal, in other words, to be Black. Where the person was supposed to go was a good question as the next state probably had a similar exclusion law.

If permission to stay was granted, which it might be if the Black person went through some legal rigamarole, he or she had to post bond guaranteeing good behavior.[8]

Disobeying Missouri's expulsion order was punishable by a $10 fine. And if the Black person still didn't leave, the penalty was 20 lashes and jail time.[9]

Similar Black exclusion laws were in force in Illinois, Ohio, Indiana, Michigan and Iowa, just to name a few. Such laws were so common, in fact, that it would be easier to list the states that didn't have them than those that did.

Oregon's version was pushed through the provisional legislative committee in June 1844 by Peter Hardeman Burnett, a 37-year-old member of a slave-owning family who'd once owned two or three slaves himself. Burnett was born in Nashville, Tennessee, and moved to Clay County Missouri with his parents as a young man in 1822.

Missouri had legal slavery in about a third of its counties and generally looked the other way in the rest of them. Clay County, now part of metropolitan Kansas City, was in an area known as "Little Dixie" because it was settled mostly by people from the upper South, many of whom brought their slaves with them. About a quarter of Clay County's inhabitants were slaves—roughly twice the percentage of the state as a whole.[10]

Young Burnett was bright and ambitious. He taught himself law and practiced it. He also ran a general store, but didn't prosper at either occupation.[11]

Facing debts he couldn't pay, he helped organize a wagon train to Oregon in 1843 with creditors at his heels. His plan was to claim land he could sell to pay his debts and recover his reputation.

One thing Burnett had in abundance, if not money, was self-confidence. And ambition.

Soon after arriving in Oregon City, he got himself elected to the seven-member Provisional Legislative Assembly where he stood out for his leadership skills and lack of scruples.

An accomplishment that would come back to haunt him was sponsoring legislation to rid Oregon of Blacks.

Burnett's "lash law," as it would be known, was part of a package aimed at expelling African-Americans, whether slave or free. The law gave slave owners who had brought their human property with them a three-year window to remove them from Oregon or the slaves would be freed. This had the perhaps-unintended consequence of legalizing slavery for three years while the owners decided what to do. They could either take their slaves back to Missouri or wherever they came from, and sell them, or lose them when the deadline passed.

But that didn't mean a freed slave could stay in Oregon. He or she became subject to the Black exclusion law. Failure to leave Oregon within a certain time limit was punishable by flogging. A constable was to administer "not less than twenty nor more than twenty-nine stripes" per session.

There was no limit on sessions.

If one whipping didn't do the trick, there would be another every six months until the free Black took the hint and left.[12]

Burnett's Lash Law passed only 5-3, however, indicating a fair amount of dissent. The next Assembly changed it from a whipping to a requirement that Blacks who remained in Oregon post bond guaranteeing good behavior.[13]

A fair question is why Burnett thought it would be to his political advantage to sponsor a lash-law in the first place. One likely answer is the Cockstock incident, an outbreak of violence blamed on two Black settlers that had occurred just weeks earlier.

A free Black settler, Winslow Anderson, had hired an Indian named Cockstock to clear some land for him in exchange for a horse. But instead of giving Cockstock the horse as promised, Anderson sold it and the land to another Black settler, James D. Saules. Cockstock asked Saules for the horse he felt was rightfully his, but Saules said he knew nothing about Anderson's deal and refused. Cockstock sought help from Elijah White, the U.S. Indian sub-agent for Oregon, but White said he had no authority to do anything. The truth is that White was afraid of Cockstock who'd recently threatened to kill him over some other matter. As far as White was concerned, Cockstock was a mentally unbalanced hothead with an explosive temper and a track record of going after people with a knife.

Cockstock went to Saules' place and stole the horse. Then he got drunk and led a half-dozen other Indians into Oregon City wearing warpaint and carrying guns they pointed at people in the streets. They left without doing any harm except for putting the community on a war footing. When they came back, the people they'd scared were armed and ready.

George LeBreton, the young British-born Provisional secretary, tried to arrest Cockstock, who both stabbed and shot him, killing him. In the ensuing fracas, a second man was killed, and Anderson, the horse-welsher who'd caused all the trouble, smashed Cockstock's skull with a rifle butt, killing him.

Sheriff Meek arrested Saules a few weeks later, not for inciting the Cockstock violence, but for stirring up threats against the eccentric George Pickett, a self-described journalist from Virginia who advocated slavery and wrote screeds on cedar shingles that he nailed to trees.[14]

An all-white jury tried Saules, found him guilty and handed him over to Elijah White, who took him to Astoria and tried to send him away on a ship. "But the captain," White reported, "absolutely declined to take him on board."[15]

White didn't want to bring Saules back to the Willamette settlement, having no jail to incarcerate him. So, he gave Saules strict orders to stay in the Astoria area near a mission family.

"Although unsuccessful in getting employment (on the ship) as I had hoped," White wrote, "he remains in that vicinity with his Indian wife and family, conducting, as yet, in a quiet manner, but doubtless ought to be transported, together with every other negro, being in our condition dangerous subjects."[16]

Indian agents in the 1840s reported to the U. S. War Department, and White wrote to Secretary William Wilkins asking whether Blacks could be banned from coming to Oregon. Wilkins' reply, if any, is unknown. But Burnett's Lash Law and the Oregon's remoteness helped keep the Black population small.[17]

5. NOTES

1. Charles H. Carey. *General History of Oregon*, 3rd ed. Binfords & Mort, Portland OR 1971, p. 231.

2. Ibid, pp. 450-51.

3. Dorothy O. Johansen. *Empire of the Columbia*, 2nd ed. Harper & Row, NY 1967, pp. 184-85. Also see: "Document: A Narrative by Dr. McLoughlin," *Oregon Historical Quarterly*, vol. 1, 1900, pp. 195 ff.

4. Johnson's law-abiding reputation suffered a slight hitch in 1846 when he was indicted for making illegal whiskey at his sawmill on Johnson Creek, the eponymous flood-prone waterway in what would become Southeast Portland. Jim Huff, *Portland Police to 1870* (Portland Police Museum and Historical Society.) Also, Ginny Mapes, "The Oregon Encyclopedia."

5. Farnham Petition, cited by Carey, p. 318.

6. John Todd letter to Edward Ermatinger, March 10, 1845, ms. 1012 Oregon Historical Society.

7. Frances Fuller Victor. *The River of the West,* vol. 2. p 115. Mountain Press Publishing Co., Missoula MT 1985. Also see Nancy Eisenburg. *White Trash: The 400-Year Untold Story of Class in America.* Penguin Books, 2017.

8. Oregon Archives, p. 28 ff. Also see Gray, pp. 382-83, and Carey, p. 342.

9. Missouri Secretary of State archives.

10. According to the 1850 federal census 13 percent of Missouri's people were enslaved—87,442 out of 682,044.

11. https://www.legendsofamerica.com/we-oregontrailaccount/

12. Judicial whipping of both blacks and whites persisted in America until well into the 20th Century.

13. *The Oregon Archives*, p. 28 ff. Also see Gray, pp. 382-83, and Carey, p. 342.

14. Pickett was an older cousin of the future Confederate Maj. Gen. George E. Pickett, best-known for his disastrous charge at Union lines during the Battle of Gettysburg.

15. Saules had been a ship's cook with the Wilkes exploring expedition and either deserted or was shipwrecked near Astoria in 1841. That made him one of Oregon's first known Black residents.

16. Gray, p. 396.

17. Any notion that northern states were ipso facto liberal on racial matters and that Oregon was a racist outlier is mistaken. Most northern states had Black exclusion laws nearly identical to Burnett's lash law, and some tolerated outright slavery or its functional equivalent.

Free Blacks who tarried in Illinois not only could be arrested and fined repeatedly but auctioned off as laborers. The Illinois law also prescribed a lashing for Blacks who gathered in groups of three or more to dance or make "revelry." [Roger Bridges. 2015 Fall/Winter *Journal of the Illinois State Historical Society*. Also, National Public Radio WUIS.]

Ohio and Indiana did not make it illegal for Blacks to dance more than two at a time, but required them to show legal proof that they were free and to post a $500 bond guaranteeing good behavior.

Michigan also required a $500 bond and saddled free Blacks with a number of civic disabilities. It did not allow Blacks to serve on juries, attend public schools, or do anything else the Legislature found objectionable.

Indiana passed a law in 1843 saying only white children could attend public schools. A little later, it banned Black people from moving there, period. Anyone who helped them or gave them a job could be fined.

Outright slavery also existed in the north. To an extent.

Although all six Midwestern states had joined the union under the Northwest Ordinance prohibiting slavery, all found ways around it.

The Illinois Legislature decided that the Ordinance didn't apply to slaves already living in Illinois. By 1845, Illinois had a slave population of nearly 5,000.

Henry Dodge, the governor of Wisconsin, personally owned five slaves and put them to work in a lead smelter. [Davidson, J. N. *Negro Slavery in Wisconsin and the Underground Railroad*. Parkman Club Publications, 1897.]

6.
Oregon turns to Iowa

The autumn of 1844 brought another wave of immigrants to Oregon. The number of Euro-Americans grew to about 6,000, increasing the challenge of maintaining law and order.[1] Oregon lacked mature civic institutions and was still using laws borrowed from the Iowa Territory.

Among the approximately 48 crimes listed in the Iowa code, murder was the only one punishable by death as a stand-alone offense. In today's parlance it would be termed murder in the first degree, defined as "the unlawful killing of a human being in the peace of the United States, with malice aforethought either expressed or implied."

The law gave examples of how a murder of that sort might occur. It listed "poisoning, starving, drowning, stabbing, shooting, or by any other of the various forms or means by which human nature may be overcome and death thereby occasioned."

To get a conviction, the prosecutor had to show that the murder was done with "express malice"—the "deliberate intention unlawfully to take away the life of a fellow creature, which is manifested by external circumstances capable of proof."

Malice "shall be implied," the statute said, "when no considerable provocation appears, or when all the circumstances of the killing show an abandoned and malignant heart. The punishment of any person convicted of the crime of murder shall be death."

Death, as a matter of fact, was the only sentence the Provisional government was prepared to carry out since Oregon had no prison.

Manslaughter and other lesser degrees of murder drew five-year sentences but it was unclear how that would work in prison-less Oregon.

A substantial section of the law was devoted to "Excusable Homicide." Peace officers and citizens alike were excused if they happened to kill a suspected felon while trying to make an arrest. It didn't matter whether the person killed was a suspected serial killer or a shoplifter as long as the crime was a felony.

Hangmen who carried out death sentences were specifically immunized. Excuses also were available for people in positions of authority who might accidentally kill someone in their charge. "A parent moderately correcting a child, or a master his servant or student, or an officer punishing a criminal," were examples cited in the law.

So, it was perfectly all right in Oregon to beat someone to death as long as the beating was "moderate."

But "if a parent or master exceed the bounds of moderation, or the officer the sentence under which he acts, either in the manner, the instrument, or quality of punishment, and death ensue, it will be manslaughter, or murder, according to the circumstances of the case," the law said.[2]

Besides premeditated murder, three other crimes were capital if someone got killed during their commission, even if unintentionally. The specific crimes were arson, robbery, burglary, and perjury leading to the death of an innocent person.

Several kinds of offenses against persons could get the perpetrator a life sentence. They included dueling, mayhem, rape, homosexuality, having sex with an animal, and attempted poisoning. "Attempted poisoning" seemed to refer mostly to abortion. It included using a substance to try to induce a "miscarriage." The penalty was up to three years' imprisonment and a $1,000 fine.

Trying to murder someone with poison, as ordinarily thought of, drew a minimum sentence of two years and a maximum of 20.

A "Crime Against Nature"—same-sex or having sex with an animal—was punishable by two to 20 years in prison.

"Mayhem"—disfiguring somebody by biting off a nose or an ear, for example—could get the perpetrator 10 years and a $3,000 fine.

Rape, especially of a minor, also drew a big-time penalty. "Every male person of this territory of the age of fourteen years and upwards who shall have carnal knowledge of any female child under the age of ten years, either with or without her consent, shall be adjudged guilty of the crime of rape, and upon conviction thereof, shall be punished by imprisonment for a term of not less than twenty years, and may extend to life. Any person above the age of fourteen years, who shall have carnal knowledge of any woman forcibly and against her will, shall be deemed guilty of a rape, and, upon conviction thereof, shall be punished by imprisonment not exceeding ten years, and fined not exceeding five hundred dollars."

Assault with intent to murder was punishable by a 20-year sentence and a $2,000 fine. False Imprisonment—locking somebody up without legal authority—drew up to two years and a $2,000 fine. Kidnapping drew 10 years and a $1,000 fine.

Nine specific crimes were punished not just with a prison sentence but with a virtual Scarlet Letter. Perpetrators were declared "infamous."

The code read:

> Each and every person in this Territory who may hereafter be convicted of the crime of rape, kidnapping, wilful and corrupt perjury, arson, burglary, robbery, sodomy, or the crime against nature, larceny, forgery, counterfeiting, or bigamy, shall be deemed infamous, and shall forever thereafter be rendered incapable of holding any office of honor, trust, or profit, of voting at any election, of serving as a juror, and of giving testimony in this Territory.

A single person marrying somebody else's wife or husband—not to be confused with bigamy—could be sentenced to a year's imprisonment and a $500 fine. But the culprit wasn't branded as "infamous."

Certain kinds of popular crimes came with generous loopholes.

Men and women caught cohabiting without benefit of wedlock could escape a fornication charge by getting married.

Lewdness, though, couldn't be wriggled out of so easily. It could draw some jail time. The definition of lewdness was any "notorious act of public indecency tending to debauch the public morals." It included "keeping a place for the practice of fornication"—a no-tell hotel, for example—or any "common, ill-governed, and disorderly house for the encouragement of idleness, gaming, drinking, fornication, or other misbehavior."

That meant bordellos and gambling dens.

Surprisingly, the criminal code included a pioneering environmental protection law. "Obstructing Public Roads &c.," as the law was titled, made it a crime to

> dump obnoxious material into any public river, or stream declared navigable by law or to continue such obstruction so as to render the same inconvenient or dangerous to pass, or shall erect or establish any offensive trade, or manufactory, or business, or continue the same after it has been erected or established, or shall in anywise pollute any water course, lake, pond, marsh, or common sewer, or continue such pollution so as to render the same offensive or unwholesome to the county, town, village, or neighborhood thereabouts.

Its main intent was to regulate slaughterhouses and tanneries and other businesses known for making a mess. Violators could be fined up to $100.

Another law prohibited digging up a corpse

for the purpose of dissection, or any surgical or anatomical experiment, or for any other purpose, without the knowledge and consent of the near relatives of the deceased, or shall in any way aid, assist, counsel, or procure the same to be done. Every such person so offending shall, on conviction, be fined not less than one hundred dollars nor more than five hundred dollars.

A list of crimes deemed injurious to civil order and responsibility included voting more than once in an election, refusing to join a posse, and defacing a public notice. Fines began at $75.

The code also addressed "Cheats, Swindlers &c.," who, for example, used phony documents to sell property they didn't own, or who obtained:

> anything of value by misrepresenting or causing others to misrepresent someone's honesty, wealth, or mercantile character.
>
> Every such offender shall be deemed a swindler, and, on conviction, shall be sentenced to return the property so fraudulently obtained, if it can be done, and shall be fined in a sum not less than one hundred dollars, nor more than one thousand dollars, or imprisoned at hard labor not less than two years, nor more than five years, or both, at the discretion of the court.

Another kind of scoundrel the law emphatically disapproved of was the "Common Cheat," a prime example being millers who "shall knowingly sell by false weight or measures, or shall knowingly use false measures at any mill in taking toll for grinding corn, wheat, rye, or other grain."

"Common Cheats" were subject to two years imprisonment and a $500 fine.

"Fraudulent and Malicious Mischief" covered a long list of misdeeds including destroying a house, breaking doors and windows, setting fire to a haystack, girdling a shade tree, running a carriage into a slough, and killing somebody's dog or heifer. The penalty for fraudulent and malicious mischief was up to four months in jail and a $200 fine.

A sub-category of bad deportment was "damaging or destroying a jail." The penalty was a maximum fine of $5,000 or the cost of the jail. No jail time was prescribed, however, for obvious reasons.

Finally, the code specified how criminal sentences were to be carried out.

> The punishment of death shall be by hanging the person convicted by the neck until dead at such time as the court shall direct, which time shall not be less than fifteen, nor more than twenty-five days from the time sentence is pronounced, unless for good cause the court or Governor may prolong the time; and the court, at their discretion, may order such execution to take place in public or private. If the latter, the court shall appoint twelve respectable citizens of the county to see that the sentence of the law is faithfully executed.

The corpse of the executed criminal could also be punished.

Section 102 of the code, titled "The Body of the Criminal for Dissection," said "The court may order on application of any respectable surgeon or surgeons, that the body...be delivered to such surgeon or surgeons for dissection."

The code also gave specific instructions as to what could and could not be done with prisoners sentenced to prison. They could be put to work on public roads, for instance, as long as they were kept shackled and under surveillance.

"It shall be lawful, and is made the duty of the sheriff or keeper of any such convicts," said the law, "to secure them, without cruelty, by ball and chain, or block, and also to have a sufficient guard to prevent their escape."

Prisoners could be held indefinitely if they didn't or couldn't pay their fines. Poverty was not an excuse. The law did not distinguish between willful refusal and lack of ability, which in practical terms meant imprisonment for debt even though it was no longer legal in the United States, at least at the federal level.

Congress abolished imprisonment for debt in 1833 but left it to the states to make their own rules. By 1849, a dozen states followed the federal example and the practice fell into disuse even if antique laws lingered on the books here and there. Bankruptcy laws proved more productive for getting creditors paid while giving the people who owed them money a chance at a fresh start.

It was not until 1970 that the U.S. Supreme Court ruled that prisoners couldn't be kept longer than their maximum sentence even if they still owed fines. A few years later the court modified the ruling to distinguish between those who couldn't pay and those who simply refused.

Other types of debtors could still be thrown in the clink though, such as evaders who didn't pay their income taxes or deadbeats who didn't pay court-ordered child support.[3]

Among the many curious crimes in Oregon's early criminal code was failure to look respectable:

> Every person who does, or is suspected to, get his livelihood by gaming, and every able-bodied person who is found loitering, and wandering about, and not having wherewithal to maintain himself, by some visible property, and who doth not betake himself to labor, or some honest calling, to procure a livelihood, and all persons who may become chargeable to the county, and all other idle, vagrants, dissolute persons, rambling about, without any visible means of subsistence, shall be deemed, and considered, as vagrants.

Adult vagrants were to be jailed and could be hired out for labor, with their earnings going to pay any debts they might have. If they didn't have any, the money went to the county treasury.

A vagrant minor could be bound out to learn a useful trade. When the minor reached age 21, the sheriff had the option of hiring him out for up to nine months, with his earnings applying to any debts he might have. The rest were returned to him to help him get a new start. The vagrancy laws for minors were conspicuously progressive for their era, placing more emphasis on rehabilitation than punishment.

Although land disputes remained the most common source of trouble in the new colony, a growing population made things more complicated. McLoughlin reported that several known outlaws had arrived with the latest wagon train. He said,

> at a Methodist camp meeting one of the new Immigrants (whom they say was converted) got up and confessed publicly that he belonged to a band of Robbers in the State of Arks-ans-as, that there were several of his former associates in the Country, that if they reformed he would not divulge their names, but if they did anything he would.[4]

CRIMES AND PUNISHMENTS IN MID-1840s OREGON
* Maximum punishment

Murder	Death
Manslaughter	5 years
Dueling	$2,000
Attempt to Poison	20 years*
Abortion	3 years*
Mayhem	10 years
Child rape	Life*
Adult rape	10 years*
Crime against nature	20 years
Attempted murder	3 years*
False imprisonment	2 years
Kidnapping	10 years
Arson	10 years
Burglary	7 years
Robbery	5 years
Larceny	5 years
Horse stealing	10 years
Hog stealing	5 years
Receiving stolen goods	10 years
Officer embezzling	10 years
Altering deeds	5 years
Removing land marks	3 months
Servant embezzling	5 years
Bailee conversion	5 years
Lodger embezzling	5 years
Misprision of felony	3 years
Counterfeiting coin	10 years
Possessing counterfeit	10 years
Faking official seals	7 years
Perjury causing death	Death

Bribery	3 year
Oppression by jailer	Firing + $500
Resisting legal server	Beating
Rescue post-conviction	20 years
Rescue pre-conviction	3 years
Helping jail escape	2 years
Helping custody escape	1 year
Officer refusing to arrest	6 months
Conspiracy	1 year
Jury tampering	2 years
Official extortion	$200
Blackmail	1 year
Rioting	6 months
Libeling a dead person	2 years
Bigamy	5 years
Adultery & Fornication	1 year
Lewdness	1 year
Water pollution	$100
Disinterring a body	$500

6. NOTES

1. Native Americans still greatly outnumbered the white settlers, with estimates ranging as high as 50,000.

2. "An officer punishing a criminal" apparently referred to corporal punishment ordered by a court in lieu of imprisonment or to enhance a prison sentence. But the "moderation" rule still applied, and the officer couldn't just beat his prisoner to death by means that were immoderate.

3. Eli Hager. *Debtors' Prisons Then and Now: FAQ.* Published by the Marshall Project, 2015.

4. McLoughlin's letters, 2nd series, p. 33.

7.
Peacekeepers and jail pork

While the pioneer community waited for a jail to be built, it had to depend on peacekeepers like Joseph L. Meek.

The provisional government selected him as sheriff—Oregon's first, or perhaps the second, although the first "High Sheriff," William Johnson, left no record of his accomplishments, if any.

"A rowdy giant," is the way one neighbor described Joe Meek. He was an authentic character, memorably tough and fearless even by frontier standards.

He was an in-law of President James K. Polk and wasn't shy about letting people know it. He was born in Washington County, Virginia, and came to Oregon by way of Tennessee and the Rocky Mountains. He'd made a living for a number of years trapping beaver in the upper Columbia and Snake watersheds, managing some improbable adventures among the Blackfeet. Somewhere along the line he married a Nez Perce woman. In fact, he married three, one at a time.

When the fur trade played out, Meek moved to the Willamette Valley to farm and figure out his next move. He loved to share a jug with neighbors and regale them with an endless supply of cock-a-doodling yarns about his life as a mountain man.

One he liked to tell was how he battled a pack of rabid wolves on the Green River in Wyoming, surviving their slavering bites thanks to the medicinal properties of moonshine whiskey to which he'd remained loyal ever since.

Despite his nonsense, Meek was intelligent, literate and had good judgment, knowing when to cajole, when to order, and when to shoot. He was an easy choice for sheriff, a position he readily accepted, glad to avoid the humdrum life of a farmer.

Meek became a familiar sight as he rode around the territory with a pistol tucked in his belt, his hard-worn frock-coat left open to show he was armed, his ensemble complete with top hat and vest.[1]

Meek and his handful of constables made several arrests notable enough to be of record. One was James Conner, a moonshiner whose customers may have included Meek himself. Meek took him into custody Oct. 2, 1844, for challenging the Rev. Elijah White to a duel. White's offense, apparently, was leading a raid on Conner's still.[2]

What became of Conner isn't clear.

John Edmunds, a Meek constable, tried to serve an arrest warrant on one Joel Turnham, a reputed outlaw from Missouri, who unwisely resisted arrest. Edmunds put three bullet holes in Turnham's head, obviating the need for incarceration or trial.[3]

Meek himself served a warrant on a local hothead named Marvin R. Alderman, a Hudson's Bay employee, to answer a charge of jumping the land claim of Dougal McTavish, a fellow Company man. Alderman was arraigned before Provisional Magistrate William P. Dougherty on Oct. 15, 1844, but the outcome was not recorded.[4]

Meek sought Alderman again, later, with a warrant charging him with trying to shoot Jacob Hawn, a millwright also from Missouri. And soon after that, Meek went after Alderman with yet another warrant, based on a complaint sworn out by John McLoughlin himself, accusing Alderman of jumping the land claim of McLoughlin's brother, David.[5]

No American jail or prison existed in Oregon before 1845, so all Marshal Meek could do was serve arrest warrants and summon people to court. In most cases, the only possible punishment was a fine.

Conner, the do-it-yourself whiskey maker, couldn't be locked up for moonshining so he was fined $500.

Meek never arrested a British subject, so far as the record shows, but an American named McLame did get thrown into the Fort Vancouver jail sometime prior to 1846.

William H. Gray, the pioneering former missionary and practicing busybody, recalled that the charge against McLame was jumping a Hudson's Bay employee's land claim. For that little caper he was put in irons and detained at the Fort overnight.[6]

Gray said the politically sensitive arrest was authorized by James Douglas, McLoughlin's old enforcer who'd just replaced McLoughlin as chief factor. Although Douglas was authorized by the Americans to act as justice of the peace at Vancouver, he was uneasy about jailing an American and consulted with Gray who advised him to get rid of the case in a hurry. Douglas released McLame immediately and compensated him.[7]

The Americans' effort to establish law-and-order included a large component of crime prevention, not just punishing criminals.

The Provisional Assembly passed a law June 24, 1844, to ban liquor from the territory. The "Act to prohibit the Manufacture and Sale of Ardent Spirits" declared that alcohol would

> bring withering ruin upon the prosperity and prospects of this interesting and rising community, by involving us in idle and dissolute habits, inviting hither swarms of the dissipated inhabitants of other countries, checking immigration, destroying the industry of the country, bringing upon us the swarms of savages now in our midst, interrupting the orderly and peaceable administration of justice, and, in a word, producing and perpetuating increasing and untold miseries that no mind can rightly estimate.[8]

However, the Act provided a loophole the size of a covered wagon by saying it "should not be so construed as to prevent any practicing physician from selling such liquors for medicine, not to exceed one gallon at a time.[9]

McLoughlin owed his restored fortunes to the new government and showed his appreciation by donating two valuable lots in Oregon City for the territory's first government building, a "publick jail."[10]

Like the aid he gave the new immigrants, it was partly self-interested. The Provisional Executive Committee in December 1844 appropriated $1,500 from the heirless Ewing Young estate to finance the project, and McLoughlin hoped to get some of the money himself by selling construction materials.

The "publick goal" —as McLoughlin misspelled gaol, meaning "jail"—was so perilously close to being a boondoggle that the Executive Committee labored to justify it.

"Although the community has suffered very little as yet for the want of such a building, and perhaps another year might pass without it being occupied, which it is hoped might be the case, yet we are assured that it is better policy to have the building stand without a tenant, than a tenant without a building," the Executive Committee argued in a Dec. 16, 1844 message to the Legislative Assembly.

But it didn't stop there. A jail, the committee said, not only would deter crime (which it had just described as nearly non-existent) but also scare loafers and other unsavory sorts into mending their ways.

"To promote industry and the peace and welfare of the citizens of Oregon, this government must be prepared to discountenance indolence and check vice in the bud,[11]" the Executive Committee concluded.

In other words, unable to come up with a plausible excuse to grab Young's money, the Committee pronounced itself foresighted and did it anyway.

Besides giving the Americans a place to put future prisoners, a jail promised to pump some life into the nearly non-existent local economy. Money—actual money that could be used to transact business—was so scarce that Oregon City merchant, missionary and politician George Abernethy started issuing his own. He pasted handwritten denominations on flint-rocks and accepted them at his store as currency.

With a jail project providing a reason to siphon real U.S. dollars out of Young's estate, Abernethy hoped to get his share via scrip issued to contractors by the provisional treasury. The scrip could be used to pay for building materials at Abernethy's Oregon City general store and another that McLoughlin owned in partnership with the Hudson's Bay Company. The happy store owners could then present the scrip to the provisional treasury for actual money.

McLoughlin literally laid the groundwork for getting his share of jail pork. He offered the provisional government a free building site and was not deterred when the committee picked one of his best and most expensive properties, a scenic point of land on the Willamette River between Fourth and Fifth Streets.

McLoughlin signed over the deed Dec. 20, 1844, attaching a polite note requiring that the land "revert to me when not being used as goal."

"In the mean," McLoughlin added hopefully, "will you please select a place more suited hereafter for a goal - so I may make it over to you?"[12]

The bill for erecting the jail—Oregon's first public institution—was introduced Dec. 18, 1844 by Peter Burnett and adopted by the Provisional Legislative Committee on Christmas Eve, December 24.

Things moved rapidly. Twelve days after Burnett signed, the Provisional Executive Committee took delivery of a set of jail plans drawn by the nearest thing to an architect that it could find.

Herman Ehrenberg, a German-born civil engineer and adventurer, designed the jail for a $12 fee and delivered a thick set of drawings on Jan. 5, 1845. Sheet after sheet of floor plans and elevations were accompanied by detailed specifications covering everything from the design of hinges to the security arrangements for windows, and how timbers were to be dove-tailed at the corners to make them secure, and how many plies of wood should be used in the walls and in what dimensions, and so on and so forth. And so on. Exactly.

Ehrenberg's notion of a country jail was a two-story wooden blockhouse as stout as a fresh tree stump.

It was to measure 18 feet square on the outside, but only a little over 12 feet square inside because of the thickness of the wooden walls. Although massively strong, the two-story design made it look slender, even unstable, like a two-story outhouse about to commit a somersault.

The side view had an aerodynamic flair. The steeply-pointed roof and short overhangs on a tall structure suggested a pioneer experiment in rocket science. At casual glance, it seemed possible that Ehrenberg planned to launch Oregon's convicts into outer space.

Whatever the jail's odd appearance, its strength and security were to be formidable. Getting inmates in or out wouldn't be easy, even with the help of a jailer.

No door was provided at ground-level. Prisoners would be marched up a steep flight of wooden stairs attached to the outside to reach the second story. Once there, the jailer would have to remove a padlock from a heavy door that opened through the pitched roof to let the prisoner into an entry chamber. Jailer and prisoner both would go inside, most having to duck because the slope of the roof limited the door height to 5 feet 5 inches.

The anteroom inside would have no furnishings except for a stored stepladder. A trap-door in the floor would be opened to expose the jail chamber below.

The ladder would then be poked down through the trap-door and the prisoner would have to climb down into his abode. Once inside, the jailer would withdraw the ladder, close the trap door and lock it with a double padlock.[13]

Ehrenberg's pit-like design was so strikingly odd as to invite speculation on why he chose it. One possibility is that Ehrenberg had seen a similar design in European monasteries dating from the Middle Ages.

The Cluny reform movement that swept the monasteries at that time was marked by detailed rule-making that included very specific instructions for building monastic prisons. The reformers recommended placing disobedient or criminal monks in a chamber that could be reached only by descending a ladder.[14] Although little information is available on Ehrenberg's technical training, it's not impossible that he had visited such prisons in Germany and perhaps had seen the Cluny instructions.

For Oregon's first jail, Ehrenberg specified that the two-foot-square trap door leading down into the jail be

> made of two courses of Oak Plank, three inches thick each, and well rivetted together with wrought spikes, and firmly hung with iron hinges, extending across the full width of the door, and fastened with an iron bar, passing across, and secured with staples or eye bolts, and a good strong double Padlock.

He conceded that the walls of the jail's top-floor entry chamber could be built merely of foot-square timbers, and that a two-foot-square upstairs window could be secured with a token iron grate consisting of crosshatched one-and-a-half inch and quarter-inch iron straps riveted at their intersections.

The jail chamber itself was a different matter. Ehrenberg specified that the walls consist of a three-layered sandwich of Douglas Fir timbers, all hewn from tough red heartwood. The two outer layers of the sandwich would be foot-square members spiked over an inner layer of 8x12 inch beams. Not quite satisfied with the geologic sturdiness of 32-inch walls, Ehrenberg cautioned that the timbers be interlocked at the corners "by a dovetail joint."

The plan called for two 18-inch-square windows in the jail chamber itself, one on the north side of the building and the other on the south. The windows were to be plugged with heavy iron grates consisting of eight interlocking bars. Four of the bars would be at least four inches wide and at least a half-inch thick. These bars would be rooted deeply in the wooden walls, narrow side facing the prisoner. The wide bars would have holes bored in them to allow four smaller bars an inch-and-a-half square to be threaded through, forming a grate.

Looking out through these fortified openings, the prisoner might have felt he was lucky to get air, much less plot an escape.

No detail was too small to escape Ehrenberg's notice. Writing with ant-like patience on architectural broadsheets, Ehrenberg gave instructions for everything from the size and placement of reinforcement bolts to how many nails were the minimum necessary to secure the door frame.

For the ceiling of his dungeon, he prescribed two crosshatched layers of 8x12s. The distance from floor to ceiling was to be exactly nine feet. Ehrenberg said the floor had to be made of "timbers hewed twelve inches square, laid close together in one layer, extending to the outside of the middle tier of wall, and raised no more than four inches from the solid rock." Finally, he decreed that the four corners of the jail be bolted down "sufficient to prevent the walls being raised with a lever."[15]

For a community whose leaders averred not to see much of a crime problem, the proposed structure would have stood up to Alcatraz.

Ironically, the provisional government chose as one of its construction contractors a man then under indictment for assault with the intent to commit murder.

V. W. Dawson, a burly carpenter, had gotten into a brawl and threatened Meek with a broad-axe as Meek tried to arrest him. Meek took him at gunpoint.[16]

Apparently, neither Meek nor the government carried a grudge. Dawson, still charged with assaulting the sheriff, got a job building the jail along with another carpenter, E. W. Otey.

Their Jan. 15, 1845 contract included a $2,000 performance bond guaranteed by none other than Abernethy. Dawson and Otey agreed to furnish all labor and materials for $875.[17]

The two carpenters went to work as soon as the winter rains let up. Their contract called for three scrip payments of $291.66 each, the first one due when all construction timbers had been delivered to the site.

Dawson cashed his first scrip March 8 at McLoughlin's store. Five weeks later, April 17, Dawson cashed another scrip at Abernethy's, signaling that the jail was up and enclosed.

But Dawson had to be excused from work April 22 so he could appear in court. While he waited for his assault charge to be tried, he was put on a jury that awarded 50 cents in damages to a plaintiff in a property lawsuit. Then, clambering out of the jury box and into the dock as an accused felon, Dawson was acquitted of the assault charge, but made such a pest of himself during the trial that the judge fined him $15 for contempt of court. He paid the fine in government scrip and later found solace in cost-overruns on the jail.

Ehrenberg's copious plans somehow had neglected to mention weatherboarding or suggest how the jail's occupants would be protected from wind and rain blowing through grated windows. After taking care of this, the government issued another supplemental order hiring Dawson and a new partner, Thomas Smith, to build "two iron window shutters upon the two lower windows and fasten them with two strong iron hinges each and good and sufficient clasps and staples for fastening them with a padlock."[18]

It wasn't clear whether the shutters were to be installed over the bars or in place of them. Probably the latter, since the shutters were designed to be movable. On the other hand, if permanent bars were in place, there was no obvious reason for a padlock.

The committee's original thought was to have holes bored through the shutters for light and ventilation, but someone crossed out this specification with an ink pen before signing the order July 29, 1845.[19]

When the dust finally settled, the government had spent at least $1,153.95 on its new "Public jail." This included $175, more or less, in fees the state treasurer had deducted as compensation for disbursing assets from Young's estate. The balance was spent on the jail's only known furnishing—a tub.

Whether the provisional fathers intended that the tub be used for washing clothes or washing prisoners, or for some other purpose, isn't known. But they paid four dollars for it, and recorded the seller's name as W. C. Remick.[21]

7. NOTES

1. H. E. Tobie. "Joseph L. Meek, a Conspicuous Personality." *Oregon Historical Quarterly*, vol. 1, p. 22. Also see Frances Fuller Victor. *The River of the West - The Adventures of Joe Meek*. Mountain Press Publishing Co., Missoula MT 1983 (two volumes.)

2. *Oregon Supreme Court Record*. Stevens-Ness Law Publishing Co. Portland OR, 1938, pp. 7-8.

3. Gray, p. 389. Also, Carey's *General History of Oregon*, pp. 321-22, above.

4. Tobie, p. 26.

5. Ibid. Also of note was a newcomer to the territory, Alex R. Stoughton, who was arrested, convicted and fined $25 for "assault with intent to inflict great bodily harm." [*Oregon Supreme Court Record* (Stevens-Ness Law Publishing Co.: Portland, 1938), p. 8.] Stoughton was on his way to becoming Oregon's first documented career criminal, failing the good-citizenship test over and over again for the rest of his life. After moving to Marion County around 1850, Stoughton was indicted repeatedly for theft including one case in which his own son testified against him. In 1882, at age 75, he was listed as an inmate of the Columbia County Jail. Thirteen years after that—he would have been nearly 90—he turned up on the convict roster at Oregon State Penitentiary.

6. It may have been David McLoughlin's claim.

7. Gray, pp. 196-97.

8. Cited by Gray, p. 369.

9. Gray, p. 394.

10. "Public jail" was the phrase used by Osborn Russell and P. G. Stewart, signing for the fledgling government's executive committee. Considering the long Anglo history of privately-owned jails, attaching "public" to "jail" wasn't necessarily redundant.

11. *The Oregon Archives*, pp. 57-58.

12. Cited by Young, *Oregon Historical Quarterly*, vol. 21, 1920, p. 312.

13. Territorial document No. 13006, Oregon State Archives.

14. *Imprisonment In Medieval England*. Ralph B. Pugh. Cambridge University Press, 1968, pp. 375-76. The pit-like design of monastic prisons as prescribed by medieval reformers at Cluny required access solely by ladder and forbade windows. The reasons, probably, were more theological than architectural, making it reasonable to look in the Bible to see what may have inspired the monks. On one hand, the Clunian carcer resembled the pits of Tartarus to which God was said to have consigned the devil and his rebellious cohorts (Peter 2: 3-4); but on the other hand, there were clearer scriptural references to innocent or holy men being put into pits by jealous schemers. The prophet Jeremiah was lowered into Mirv cistern for his unwelcome preaching (Jeremiah 38:5). Joseph's brothers put him in a cistern out of jealousy (Genesis 37: 22-24). If the pit-type jail was lifted from scripture, it's possible that the Clunyites were as much issuing a reminder to the jailers as creating an unpleasant environment for the prisoners.

15. Territorial document No. 13006, Oregon State Archives.

16. Peter H. Burnett. "Recollections of an Old Pioneer." *Oregon Historical Quarterly*, vol. 5, pp. 167-68. Dawson was indicted Oct. 23, 1844. See *Oregon Supreme Court Record*, Book No. 1, 1844-1848.

17. Oregon territorial documents 745, 445, 475, 524 ff, and 1035.

18. Ibid.

19. Ibid.

21. F. G. Young. "Finances of the Provisional Government." *Oregon Historical Quarterly*, vol. 7, 1906, p. 399.

John McLoughlin, the wild-haired, fiery eyed chief factor of the Hudson's Bay Company at Fort Vancouver.
He spearheaded building the first jail in the Oregon Territory.
(Photo courtesy Oregon Historical Society.)

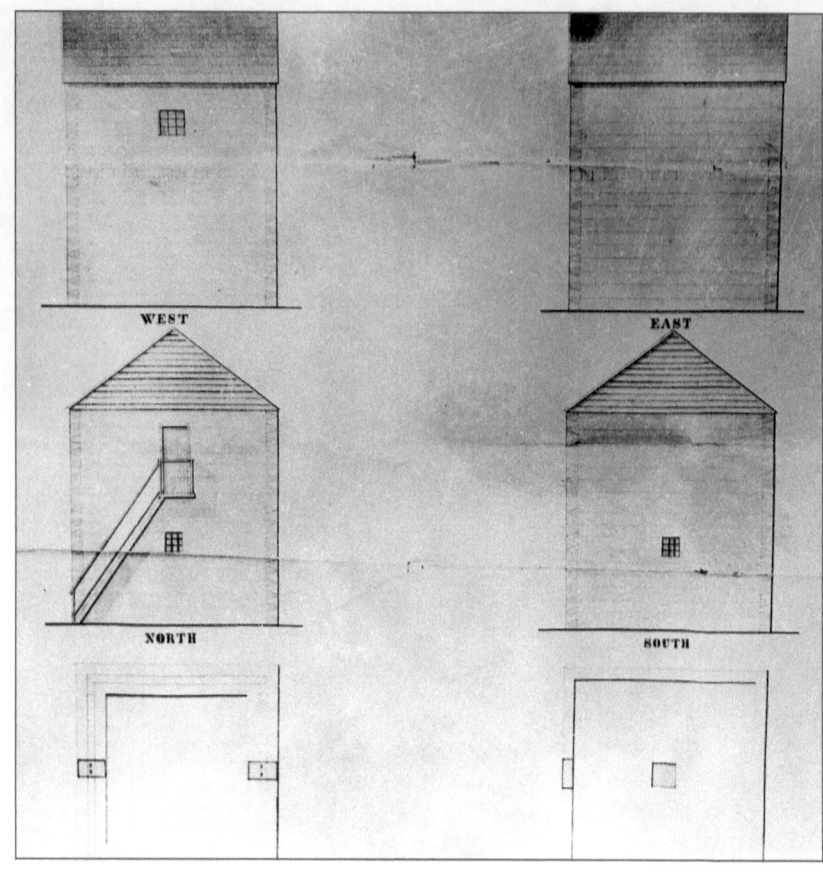

The first jail in Oregon was located near the Willamette River in Oregon City. It was a two-story wood-plank box just big enough for one prisoner. Not surprisingly someone burned it down shortly after it was built.
(Image courtesy Oregon Historical Society.)

Joe Meek, the whiskey-chugging mountain man and Oregon Territory's first federal marshal. He presided over the territory's first official execution: five Cayuse Indians convicted in the Whitman Mission murders. (Photo courtesy Oregon Historical Society.)

A posse of volunteers was occasionally assembled to run down criminals in the Oregon Territory who tried to escape justice.
(Undated photo courtesy Oregon Historical Society.)

Oregon's first penitentiary was located in Portland. The institution was moved to Salem in 1866 and the city recouped some of its money by selling the building to Oregon Ironworks for $6,000.
(Image courtesy Oregon Historical Society.)

The penitentiary (blocky, rectangular building right of center) straddled Blocks 106 and 107 in downtown Portland roughly where the Marquam Bridge today crosses to the west side of the Willamette River.

(Opposite) Portland's prison is identified by the photographer as "3." (1867 photo/key by Carlton Watkins, courtesy Oregon Historical Society.)

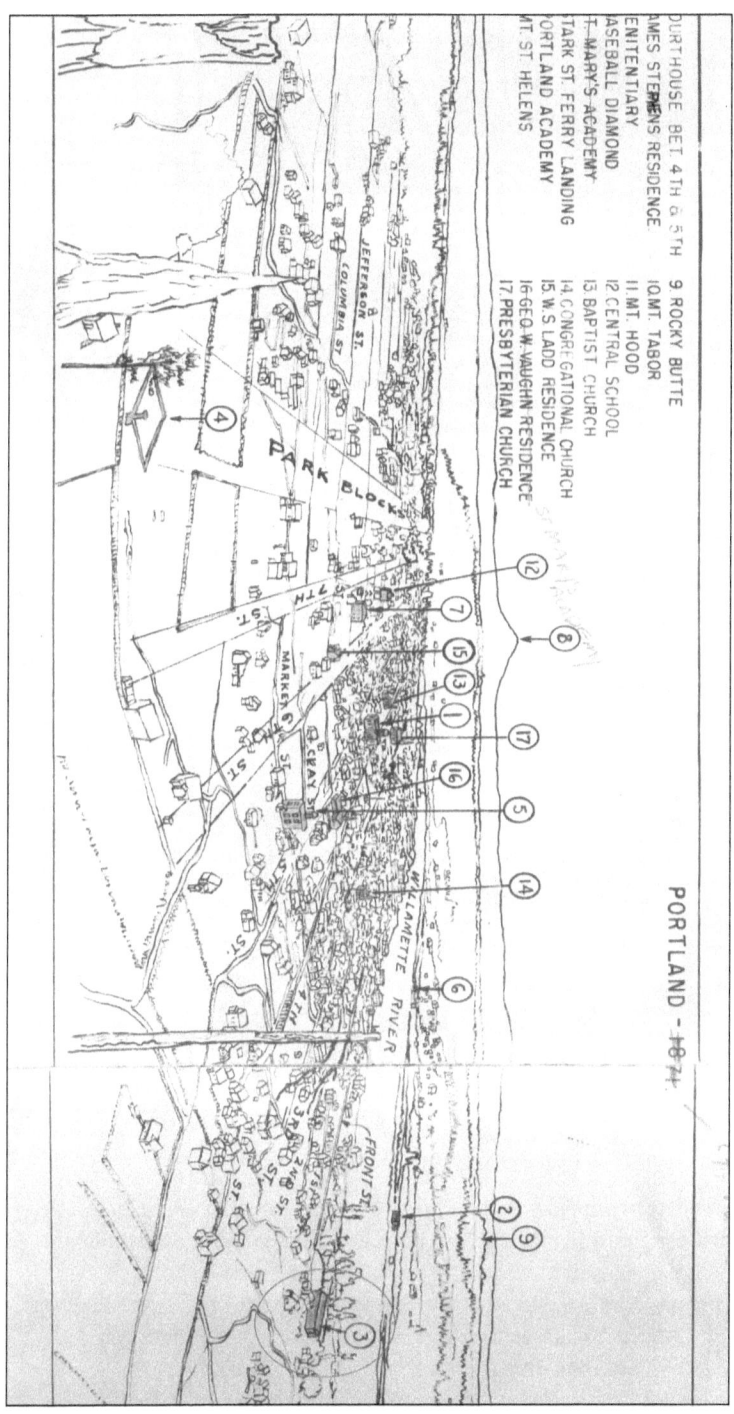

Convict Record Oregon Penitentiary

No.	NAME	COUNTY	CRIME	SENTENCE (YEARS / MOS.)	RECEIPT
1	Charley Indian	Marion	Larceny	3	
2	Sharp Cornelius	Clackamas	Murder in 2d Degree	Life	Feb 15th 1854
3	W. Lair William	Linn	Murder in 2d Degree	Life	Feb 15th 1854
4	Sturr Patrick	Jackson	Assault with int to kill	10	May
5	O'Kelly Nimrod	Benton	Murder		
6	Noll William	Linn	Assault with int to kill	2	May 21st 1854
7	Jim Oison	Clackamas	Arson	11	July 15th 1854
8	Lamb Charity	Clackamas	Murder in 2d Degree	Life	Sept 15th 1854
9	Marsh James	Washington	Assault with int to kill	3	Dec 7th 1854
10	Weston Geo H	Clackamas	Larceny	1	March 10th 1855
11	Marks Joseph	Washington	Larceny	3	April 1st 1855
12	Williams Jack H	Multnomah	Riot	1	May 8th 1855
13	Miller John	Jackson	Assault with int to kill	2	May 29th 1855
14	Quinn John	Clackamas	Burglary	1	Oct 20th 1855
15	Hill John	Multnomah	Larceny	6	July 6th 1856
16	Eck Rufus E.	Multnomah	Manslaughter	2	July 16th 1856
17	Stots Charles	Polk	Manslaughter	10	Dec 31 1856
18	Eddins Wm W.	Linn	Larceny	2	May 1st 1857
19	Komosko Jim	Clatsop	Burglary	3	May 23rd 1857
20	Gill Jean	Jackson	Assault with int to kill	5	June 21 1857
21	Livingston George	Jackson	Assault with int to kill	11	June 29th 1857
22	Stuart Clark	Multnomah	Larceny	3	Oct 9th 1857
23	Noy Edward E	Multnomah	Larceny	3	Nov 9th 1857

The first prisoners listed at Oregon's new penitentiary were not necessarily the first criminals to be put in jail in Oregon, but it was the first time the state tried to be organized about its new institution.
Inmates were listed in what was known as the prison's "Great Register." Convict No. 8 was Charity Lamb, Oregon's first female inmate.
(Ca. 1854. Image courtesy Oregon Historical Society.)

Prison guards, officials and their families at Oregon's new penitentiary in the new state capitol: Salem. Most everyone who worked at the prison—and their families—lived on-site.
(Ca. late 1870s. Photo courtesy Oregon Historical Society.)

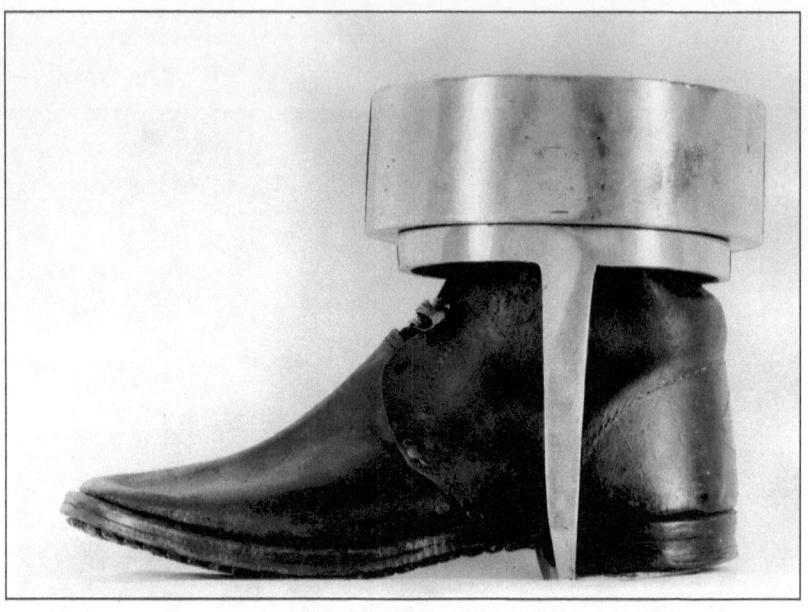

Oregon's prison became infamous in 1866 when Warden J. C. Gardner invented the Gardner Shackle or "Oregon Boot." It was meant to prevent prisoner escapes, but it also prevented them from walking and sleeping normally.
(Photo courtesy Oregon Historical Society.)

8.
Bad medicine

The Oregon City jail didn't last long.

On the night of August 18, 1846—about a year after Dawson and Otey finished hammering it together—someone burned it to the ground.

Fingers were pointed at the jail's one former tenant, a local eccentric named Samuel Goodhue who'd made a nuisance of himself writing inflammatory letters to the editor and signing other people's names to them.

But nothing definite could be pinned on Goodhue, so all Gov. George Abernethy could do was fume about the destruction of public property and write a report to the Territorial Assembly.

"A reward of $100 was immediately offered," he wrote, "but, as yet, the offender has not been discovered. Should you think it best to erect another jail, I would suggest the propriety of building it of large stones, clamped together."

The penny-pinching Abernethy was not eager to spend money on a clamped-stone jail or anything that grand unless the Assembly would listen to reason about the evils of liquor.

"A small building would answer all purposes for many years if we should be successful in keeping ardent spirits [liquor] out of the territory," Abernethy argued to the Assembly.

As a teetotaling former Methodist missionary, Abernethy saw liquor as the root of all evil. Or the root of an awful lot of it anyway.

Get rid of liquor, Abernethy preached, and crime would mostly disappear.

It was the same sort of argument that future politicians would make about drugs.

Abernethy was so sure he was right that he devoted a full quarter of his executive message to the urgency of suppressing liquor. Oregon's measly $100 fine for running a whiskey still and $20 for selling the product were insufficient, he complained, even though it was serious money in those days.

Abernethy's faith in the curative power of Prohibition wasn't entirely crazy, but Oregon was changing fast. Settlers arriving by the thousands didn't always share the governor's enthusiasm for sobriety.

Stalemate ensued. No new jail was built and liquor kept flowing and crime continued as usual.

Meantime, what to do with criminals and suspects was left up to localities that had to improvise. They kept them in private homes. They kept them in holes in the ground. They kept them in storerooms.

For a time, Oregon City put prisoners in a big iron box. Not much is known about it, but one account said it was large enough to accommodate two men "but not comfortably."

There is no record that the box was used much, whether it was comfortable or not. The Oregon City newspaper did mention one detainee, a drunk who galloped his horse recklessly through the streets. As soon as the man sobered up, the local paper reported, he was reprimanded and discharged.

Abernethy was out of office before Oregon's Provisional government finally replaced the original jail.

The new one wasn't exactly a jail, though, and it wasn't permanent. It was a re-purposed storeroom in a warehouse on an island in the

Willamette River at Oregon City. Abernethy owned the warehouse and either rented or lent jail space to the provisional government.

The island, now known as Abernethy Island, was an oversize sandbar immediately downstream of the one of the biggest waterfalls in North America. Willamette Falls was second only to Niagara Falls in volume of water, plunging four or five stories over a rocky ledge and into the lower river, regularly hurling logs that sometimes beached themselves on the island and provided fodder for a sawmill that the waterfall powered.

So far as is known, Abernethy Island's makeshift jail was used only once, in 1850. It held defendants in the most notorious criminal trial Oregon had ever seen.

Five Cayuse tribal leaders were charged with murdering Dr. Marcus Whitman, a medical missionary, at a place called Waiilatpu about 200 miles up the Columbia River near Fort Walla Walla. The doctor and his wife, Narcissa, and a dozen other people were shot, beaten or hacked to death over a period of several days in late November 1847.[1]

More than 50 survivors, all women and children, were held hostage until ransomed several weeks later by a Hudson's Bay negotiator. A militia of settlers and then U.S. Army regulars attacked and harried the Cayuse until they surrendered five chiefs to face trial in June 1850. One may have believed he was going to Oregon City just to give his side of the story, but it didn't turn out quite that way.

The accused were sequestered on the island to make any possible rescue attempt by friends unlikely to succeed. The warehouse normally was used for grain and lumber, but one of the storerooms made a workable jail by adding a stout padlock for the door and chains to fasten the prisoners to a wall.

On May 21, a federal grand jury in Oregon City indicted "Telakite, Tomahas otherwise called the Murderer, Clokomas, Isiaasheluckas and Kiamasumkin" for the premeditated murder of Marcus Whitman. None of the other victims was named, most likely because it was too hard to connect individual defendants with individual people who were slain. But it didn't matter that much because being found guilty of murdering just one individual, Marcus Whitman, was enough to send all five defendants to the gallows.

Telakite, spelled Tiloukaikt in later versions, told his captors that he and his fellow chiefs had surrendered to U.S. authorities to spare their tribe a war of extermination.

"Did not your missionaries tell us that Christ died to save his people? So we die to save our people," Tiloukaikt said.

The trial began May 23, 1850 and the outcome was never in serious doubt. All five were convicted and sentenced to hang. By modern standards the trial was a jamboree of reversible error.

Only white men were allowed by law to serve on the jury. Women and Indians could attend the trial as spectators but couldn't testify. And the defendants were paraded into the jam-packed courtroom—a borrowed saloon—wearing chains, a virtual neon sign to advertise guilt. All were kept in chains in view of the jury as the trial proceeded.

Presiding judge Orville C. Pratt, the first federal judge of the Oregon Territory and as crooked as a dog's hind leg, instructed the jurors they could assume the defendants' guilt because they'd been surrendered by fellow tribesmen who obviously knew the truth.

Kintzing Pritchette, Oregon's new Territorial Secretary and second-in-command to Gov. Joe Lane, was appointed chief defense counsel. He was a well-trained lawyer and practicing alcoholic whose appointment could be seen as cynical. To the astonishment of many, however, Pritchette sobered up long enough to fight a brilliant, if hopeless, battle to save his clients.

Knowing he'd never get them acquitted on the facts, he leaned hard on the law. In a series of pre-trial motions he demanded that Pratt dismiss the charges on grounds that the court lacked jurisdiction. The murders, he pointed out, occurred nearly a year before Oregon was even a U.S. territory. That, he said, meant the crimes might as well have taken place on the Moon and that U.S. law did not and could not apply. Therefore, he argued, his clients were charged illegally and had to be freed.

Pratt denied the motion. What kind of law, he scoffed, would apply at the Whitman Mission if not American law?

The answer, Pritchette said, was Cayuse law. The fact that Cayuse law was unwritten did not mean it was invalid, he argued. From time immemorial he said, the Cayuse sanctioned the killing of medicine men who failed to cure their patients—who made "bad medicine." He pointed out that Marcus Whitman had long presented himself to the Cayuse as a healer and thus subjected himself to the same tribal law as applied to other medicine men.

Dr. John McLoughlin, retired chief factor at Fort Vancouver, testified that Pritchette was correct. He said he'd warned Dr. Whitman a number of times that he was exposing himself to serious danger by practicing medicine in Cayuse country.[2]

The extended series of killings that began at the mission Nov. 29, 1847, was triggered by Marcus Whitman's failure to stem a deadly outbreak of measles. Cayuse hostility and desperation had been growing for some time. The Whitman Mission stood at the western terminus of the Oregon Trail and the Cayuse who lived there, the Waiilatpu band, were taking the brunt. They were not happy that the Whitmans spent most of their time helping the newcomers who the Cayuse saw increasingly as an existential threat.

As relations with the Cayuse neared a breaking point, Whitman journeyed East to confer with his church board. He asked to change the purpose of the Waiilatpu mission, saying he'd largely given up on the Cayuse who were not only impenitent but had gone so far as to assault him physically.

He asked permission to focus on the settlers from then on, justifying it by citing Scripture. The Cayuse, Whitman said, had failed to heed God's command to "increase and multiply and fill the Earth" and therefore had no right to complain about those who did.

As Whitman largely turned his back on them, Cayuse fears about having their homeland taken away reached a climax. What pushed them over the edge was the arrival of a stranger who found willing ears for lies he made up about the Whitmans.

Joe Lewis, who was half Indian from an eastern tribe, had shown up at Waiilatpu with an immigrant wagon train that left him behind when it departed for the Willamette Valley. Lewis no doubt was familiar with the injustices committed against Native peoples where he'd lived before. But he also had designs on the Whitmans' property and ultimately would betray Tiloukaikt to enrich himself.

At Waiilatpu he moved back and forth between the Whitman mission and the Cayuse village nearby.

At some point, as the epidemic raged, Lewis told Tiloukaikt and the other Cayuse leaders that he had proof that Whitman wasn't just failing to cure them of measles but was killing them deliberately. He claimed he'd overheard Whitman and his wife plotting to poison them to steal their land.

Marcus Whitman, he said, confided to Narcissa that he was giving sick Cayuse black pills to make them die while giving the white people white pills to cure them. He said he heard Narcissa approve of the poisonings and say she was glad he was doing it. Therefore, Joe Lewis said, Narcissa Whitman deserved to die as well.

As proof he was telling the truth, Joe Lewis pointed out that many of Marcus Whitman's white patients survived while many Cayuse died.[3]

Lewis's claims about "poison pills" might not have gained the traction it did had it not been for at least two previous incidents involving poison. Years earlier, Marcus Whitman had laced meat with strychnine to kill wolves preying on farm animals, and some Indians unknowingly took it for food and were stricken. Also, a mission gardener foolishly dosed some melons with a strong emetic to discourage thefts, making some Cayuse violently sick.

Tales casting Narcissa as a wicked accomplice may have been easier for the Cayuse to believe because they didn't much like her to begin with. They called her "haughty," and said she looked down her nose at them and didn't bother to hide it.

In letters to family in the East, Narcissa complained that the Indians tracked dirt into her house and left it full of fleas. Over time, she came up with different rules for white and Indian visitors, limiting the Cayuse to an "Indian room," which they not surprisingly found insulting.[4]

Marcus Whitman's relations with the Cayuse were contentious from the time he arrived at Waiilatpu in 1836. His bull-headed refusal to pay money for the mission site, about 150 acres that he claimed Tiloukaikt's predecessor, Chief Umtippe, had given him, was a chronic sore point. And so was his refusal to stop "talking bad" to the Cayuse, preaching hellfire sermons assuring them they were doomed to perdition for having multiple wives and other things Whitman didn't understand.

In his 11 years in Oregon, Marcus Whitman did not baptize a single Indian, not finding one he thought worthy.

Pritchette's defense of the five Cayuse headmen at trial might have been harder in one respect had U.S. attorney Holbrook charged them with all 12 murders. Unwritten Cayuse law that allowed the killing of failed *te-wats*—medicine men—did not apply to most of the victims.

Two victims were young men, sick with measles, who were dragged from their beds several days after the initial attack and beaten to death with boards. Three laborers were killed as they butchered cattle in the mission corral. A tailor fleeing his shop was chased through the yard and slain. A schoolteacher trying to fetch water for sick people trapped in an attic was caught outside and killed.

Joe Lewis personally bullied and taunted a young teenage boy for the amusement of an audience, and then shot and killed him.[5]

Pritchette couldn't have pointed to Cayuse law allowing the killing of failed medicine men as a defense for any murder besides Marcus Whitman's but it probably wouldn't have mattered.

The rough justice of the trial was not well-suited for considering fine points. Kiamasumkin maintained his innocence, saying he wasn't even there. He did not testify at trial, but spoke out several days later on the eve of his execution:

> I was up the river at the time of the massacre," he said, "and did not arrive until next day. I was riding on horseback;

a white woman came running from the house, she held out her hands and told me not to kill her. I put my hand upon her hand and told her not to be afraid. There were plenty of Indians all about. She with the other women and children (later) went to Walla Walla to Mr. Ogden's. I was not present at the murder nor was I any way concerned in it. I am innocent. It hurts me to talk about dying for nothing. Our chief told me to come down and tell all about it. Those who committed the murder are killed and dead. The priest says I must die tomorrow, if they kill me I am innocent…My Young Chief told me I was to come here to tell what I know concerning the murderers. I did not come as one of the murderers, for I am innocent. I never made any declaration to any one that I was guilty. This is the last time that I may speak.[6]

Even without hearing Kiamasumpkin's statement, at least one juror had doubts about his guilt. Jacob Hunsacker asked Pratt how to weigh the fact that no witness had placed Kiamasumpkin at the scene of the crime. Pratt brushed Hunsacker's concern aside, saying there had been testimony that "all" the defendants were seen on the mission grounds, armed, during the massacre, and that sighting was enough to convict Kiamasumkin as well.

After losing his motion for dismissal of the charges for lack of jurisdiction, Pritchette made one last desperate bid to put the law between his clients and the hangman. He asked Pratt for a continuance, a pause in the proceedings, to allow time for an appeal to the U.S. Supreme Court in Washington D.C.

Pratt denied that motion, too, and the trial went ahead, lasting but a few days.[7]

The jury took 75 minutes to reach a guilty verdict without ever leaving the courtroom.

Pratt sentenced the five defendants to hang in a week's time. Gov. Lane signed the death warrant.

Pritchette didn't give up, though. He circulated a petition asking Lane to stay the executions pending an appeal to the high court, which would have taken months. Many prominent citizens signed it, including most of the lawyers who attended the trial.

Lane promised to consider it. But he had other things on his mind. At the time he signed the death warrant he also signed a letter of resignation as governor of the Oregon Territory. The effective date was June 18, nearly two weeks after the scheduled hangings. Then he left for California without signing the stay that Pritchette asked for.

Pritchette was down to his last play.

As Territorial Secretary, Pritchette by law became acting governor when Lane was out of the Territory. So he signed the stay of execution himself and served it on Marshal Meek. But Meek refused to honor it. He said he had no proof that Lane had crossed the border into California, and therefore he had to assume that Lane was still in Oregon and was still governor.

"Pritchette," Meek later quoted himself as saying, "so far as Meek is concerned, he would do anything for you. But let us talk now like men. I have in my pocket the death warrant of them Indians signed by Gov. Lane. The Marshal will execute them men, as certain as the day arrives."

Meek's position was not entirely unreasonable. Before leaving Oregon City, Lane had said he planned to stop on the way to California and take care of some official business in southern Oregon. He hoped to broker a truce between the feuding Klickitat and Rogue tribes and also arrange a peace treaty between the Rogues and the Oregon Territory. The Rogues had killed some white travelers in the Rogue River area in reprisal for the massacre of a Rogue village by white miners.

To get those things done would take some time, as would the trip itself. That meant Joe Lane might very well still be in Oregon, as Meek argued, and would still be governor.

Meek also had personal reasons for wanting the hangings to proceed as scheduled.

Several years earlier he had sent his young daughter, Helen, to the Whitmans to be raised and educated. Her mother, a Shoshone, was no longer in the picture and Meek felt incapable of raising the little girl himself. Helen was nine years old at the time of the massacre, and died of measles and neglect while being held captive.

The condemned Cayuse spent their last days chained in the warehouse. Just hours before their execution, all five were baptized into the Catholic Church by Oregon's new archbishop, Francois Norbert Blanchet.

It was a final irony.

The Whitmans, who were Presbyterians, had battled Catholic missionaries for years and Blanchet in particular. The archbishop and an assistant, Father Auguste Veyret, visited the condemned men twice a day becoming, de facto, Oregon's first prison chaplains.

On the day of execution, they baptized all five and gave them the Catholic sacraments of Holy Communion and Confirmation before accompanying them to the gallows.[8]

The five Cayuse were hanged as a group at 2 p.m. June 3, 1850, with several hundred people watching. The gallows, built during the trial and anticipating the guilty verdict, stood near John McLoughlin's house on the south end of Oregon City. A half-dozen steps led up to a scaffold where five nooses dangled from a crossbeam. A single trap-door held up by a single rope would drop the condemned men in unison.

Meek himself acted as hangman.

> I placed (the condemned men) on the drop," he later wrote. "Here the chief who always declared his innocence, Kiamasumpkin, begged me to kill him with my knife—for an Indian fears to be hanged—but I soon put an end to his entreaties by cutting the rope which held the drop, with my tomahawk. As I said 'the Lord have mercy on your souls' the trap fell and five Cayuses hung in the air. Three of them died instantly. The other two struggled for several minutes, the Little Chief, Tomahas, the longest. It was he who was cruel to my little girl at the time of the massacre; so I just put my foot on the knot to tighten it, and he got quiet. After 35 minutes they were taken down and buried.[9]

So far, the only legal or quasi-legal executions in Oregon had been carried out against Indians, at least as documented in official records.

The first execution of a white man would occur on April 18, 1851 when William Kendall, a Salem-area homesteader, was hanged for murdering a neighbor. They'd gotten into a ruckus over some hogs. The victim, Bill Hamilton, claimed that the hogs Kendall was butchering were his. Kendall settled the argument by shooting Hamilton dead. Since Salem lacked a jail, Kendall was put in irons and lodged at another neighbor's house for two weeks to await execution. Marion County paid the sheriff $150 to perform the hanging, and another $1,800 and some-odd cents to other parties for Kendall's food and lodging.

The Cayuse trial, incidentally, was not the first capital case to be tried in Oregon by a legally-constituted court. Although far less well-known, the first occurred at Fort Steilacoom on Puget Sound in present-day Washington state. It took place in the late summer or early fall, 1849.

Steilacoom was a new American fort built in response to a commotion at neighboring Fort Nisqually, a Hudson's Bay trading post. More than a hundred Snoqualmie tribesmen had tried to push their way into Nisqually to punish a man named Lahalet who they said was abusing his wife, the daughter of a Snoqualmie chief.

In a fracas at the Fort's gate, shots were fired that killed a 26-year-old American carpenter, Leander C. Wallace, as he tried to take refuge in the Fort. Whether the shooting was an accident or intentional isn't clear. But two other Americans were wounded as was an Indian child who later died.

When word reached Gov. Lane in Oregon City, he sent the Snoqualmies a message saying the whole tribe would be held responsible if it didn't surrender the guilty parties. A U.S. Army captain, Bennett H. Hill, rolled into Steilacoom with a company of field artillery and gave Snoqualmie Chief Patkanim a choice between being bombarded with cannonballs or receiving a gift of 80 blankets for handing over the perpetrators.

Patkanim took the blankets and surrendered six Snoqualmies including his own brother, Quallawowt, and five other unfortunates named Stulharrier, Kussus, Tantam, Whyerk, and Qualthlinkyne.

While the prisoners cooled their heels in a guardhouse, most of the tribe camped around Steilacoom and traded dried salmon and baskets as they waited for the trial to start. It took nearly a month. Lane had to appoint the necessary officials and get them to Steilacoom and it took time.

Oregon's Provisional Chief Justice William P. Bryant was escorted by Joe Meek, the new U.S. marshal, and by Alonzo A. Skinner, a transplanted Ohio lawyer and future Oregon Supreme Court justice who would act as prosecutor.

All three were men of action, not prone to legal dilly-dallying. Bryant was a veteran of the Black Hawk war and had served in the Indiana Legislature. He and Skinner had switched political affiliations from liberal-leaning Whig to firebrand Democrat to qualify for patronage dispensed by Joe Lane's sponsor, President James K. Polk.

Skinner convened a grand jury almost as soon as he alit from his horse, and all six prisoners were indicted for murder. That was Monday, Oct. 1.

On Tuesday, Oct. 2, Bryant commenced trial. His courtroom was the biggest log cabin he could find, 20x20 feet, but nowhere near big enough to hold the crowd that showed up. Scores and perhaps hundreds of white settlers and as many or more Indians arrived from miles around to see what would happen. They spilled out of the cabin and into the yard, and those who couldn't see or hear what was going on got a play-by-play account passed from people inside.

By the end of the day, still Oct. 2, a jury of settlers found two of the defendants guilty and acquitted four. Judge Bryant sent Lane a letter saying he thought justice was done.

"Those who were found guilty were clearly so," he wrote, adding his opinion that the three who were acquitted were "guilty to a less degree if guilty at all."

"As to the fourth," he said, "there was no evidence against him and all the witnesses swore that they did not see him during the affray or attack on Fort Nisqually. It is not improbable that he was a slave whom the guilty chiefs expected to place in their stead as a satisfaction for the American murdered."

Bryant told the acquitted defendants they were free to go, and then delivered a stern lecture to the spectators, mostly Indians. American courts, he said, were not the least interested in sacrificing somebody's slave as recompense for murder. Anyone who committed murder in U.S. territory would have to do his own swinging.

Marshal Meek hanged Quallawowt and Kussus the next day, Oct. 3, and he and Bryant and Skinner returned to Oregon City.

Bryant's report on the trial to the governor included an expense account totaling $2,379.54, including the cost of the 80 blankets.[10]

8. NOTES

1. Oregon Historical Society Research Library, file #1203 (Cayuse Five Trial Documents.)

2. Letter to the Catholic Sentinel Jan. 30 1879, p. 3, quoted by Ruby and Brown in *The Cayuse Indians: Imperial Tribesmen of Old Oregon*. Pacific Northwest National Parks and Forests Association. 1972, p. 289.

3. Today it would probably be understood that the whites were more likely to survive because previous exposure to the virus gave them a degree of immunity, while it was new to the Cayuse and more likely to prove deadly.

4. Vermin were a common problem on the frontier and not just for Indians. In letters home from the mission, Narcissa asked for fine-toothed combs for combing lice nits out of hair.

5. Lewis was never brought to justice although he did more than anyone to cause the massacre and lead the Cayuse into an unwinnable war. Then he capped off his disservice with pure treachery. Assuring Tiloukaikt that he could get guns from the Mormons in Utah in exchange for horses, he set out with several companions including Tiloukaikt's son, Painted Shirt, then murdered them along the way, stole the horses and fled to California.

6. See 1 above.

7. George Gibbs, a Harvard-trained lawyer who witnessed the trial, excoriated the judge and prosecutor in a letter home. "The Chief Justice Pratt," he wrote, "is a swindler who was whipped publicly in San Francisco by Dr. - Griffin & only escaped it here by abject cowardice. The Attorney Gen does not know the first word of law."

8. Another character of Oregon's early frontier was Francois Blanchet, a French-Canadian who'd spent years as a missionary to the Micmac and Acadian Indians of in northern Canada as well as other tribes in the Pacific Northwest.
It was legendary that Blanchet had nearly been rejected for the priesthood because he was a poor student and particularly deficient in Latin. When he somehow made it to ordination, the bishop of Montreal considered him too much of a bumpkin for a city parish. He sent him as far away as possible - to the icy woods of Canada's maritime region. When Pope Gregory XVI issued

an order out of the blue naming Blanchet as an Apostolic Vicar and then as archbishop of Oregon, some in the Canadian hierarchy thought it must be a mistake. But it was not.

Blanchet spoke several Indian languages as well as English and French, and knew Native cultures well, adapting his teachings accordingly. The vast new Oregon archdiocese was divided into three parts with Francois Blanchet presiding at Oregon City and his brother, Augustin, as bishop of the diocese of Walla Walla, and Francois's longtime fellow missionary, Modeste Demers, as bishop of Vancouver Island.

Blanchet died in 1883 and is buried in St. Paul Cemetery in St. Paul, Oregon. [From various sources including Clifford M. Drury, available at www.nps.gov/whmi/learn/historyculture/drury-book.htm.; *O'Kelly v. Territory,* 1 OR 51 (1853); *The Cayuse Indians* by Robert H. Ruby and John A. Brown, University of Oklahoma Press 1972.]

9. From "Joseph L. Meek, a Conspicuous Personality." *Oregon Historical Quarterly*, op. cit.

10. W. P. Bonney. *History of Pierce County Washington*. Pioneer Historical Publishing Co., Chicago 1927, pp. 54-58.

9.
A reasonable place

Having to serve as bailiff and hangman at Steilacoom must have been a comedown for Meek who'd recently swanned around Washington as "envoy extraordinary and minister plenipotentiary from the Republic of Oregon."

President James K. Polk, Meek's kinsman, had opened doors for him and fast-tracked his request to make Oregon a U.S. Territory. Polk signed the Enabling Act that Congress had passed in August 1848 and appointed Meek U.S. marshal. For territorial governor Polk chose Joe Lane, an Indiana politician, fellow Democrat and Mexican war veteran.[1]

Lane arrived in Oregon as a ready-made hero with leadership talent and boundless ambition. He had served as a breveted major general in the Mexican War that added California and the American Southwest to the United States.

Setting up shop in Oregon City, Lane officially proclaimed Oregon a U.S. Territory. It included not just the present-day state, but the future states of Washington and Idaho and parts of Montana and Wyoming.

Oregon was bigger than Texas.

As the new governor, Lane wasted no time establishing his authority. He sent word to the Cayuse that they could either surrender the parties responsible for the Whitman massacre or face a war of annihilation. It was the same tactic he'd used at Steilacoom and it got the same results.

As soon as five Cayuse leaders were sent to Oregon City, tried for murder and duly hanged, Lane resigned his governorship and joined the California gold rush. He was looking not just for riches but for bigger opportunities on a bigger political stage.

Lane's brief tenure would be the last hurrah for Oregon City. The old capital already was being eclipsed by an upstart rival a dozen miles up the Willamette River.

Portland wasn't yet incorporated officially as a city when it became the biggest in the Northwest. Soon it would be home to the grandest government building west of St. Louis, a territorial penitentiary. Its only possible rival would be California's San Quentin Prison, which opened in 1852 while Oregon was still making do with borrowed or makeshift jails.

Oregon at mid-century was hard-pressed to know what to do with serious lawbreakers. They either escaped justice for lack of anyone to arrest them, or were kept in county lockups, or boarded with willing landlords, or were confined by whatever means was at hand.

The Oregon City Spectator reported on Thursday, November 7, 1850 that

> ...the case of Pressie was tried and resulted in his conviction for manslaughter; he was sentenced to close imprisonment for seven years and until a prison (is built) is prepared to be kept in irons. No other cases were tried by the jury, it being impossible to find a sufficient number of persons competent to serve as jurors in the country.

California doubtlessly needed a penitentiary more than Oregon. The Golden State in 1850 had a population of 92,597 versus Oregon's 13,294.

Oregon actually had lost population in the late 1840s because of the Gold Rush. Men left their farms and jobs and ran south to join the frenzied hunt. California wasn't the only destination, either. The discovery of gold in southern Oregon ignited a riot of greed every bit as crazy as California's.

The parties responsible for Oregon's version of the Gold Rush were two characters named John Poole and James Clugage.

Exactly how they did it depends on which version of the story is true. In Version No. 1, the two partners, doing business as Jackass Freight, headed south for California with a string of pack-mules and camped in a gulch near present-day Jacksonville. As they dug a waterhole for their mules, supposedly, they unearthed gold nuggets in the gravel.

In Version No. 2, Clugage and Poole camped at the homestead of Alonzo Skinner, an Indian agent, and learned that Skinner's son and an employee named Sykes had found gold in nearby Jackson Creek. Clugage and Poole went to the creek the next day and also found gold. A lot of it.

Then the freightmen did two unusual things.

First, they filed land claims, not just mining claims, totaling nearly 500 acres. Then they publicized their gold strike instead of keeping it secret. They knew from experience that at least as much money, if not more, could be made from selling real estate and mining supplies as from mining gold.

To help things along, the two partners laid out the town of Jacksonville and watched it grow until the gold ran out, which it soon did. Meanwhile they made a fortune, very little of it from mining.[2]

Early Jacksonville was much like any other mining camp masquerading as a city. Saloons were big business, and there was little in the way of law enforcement. A man not wearing a six-shooter in the street was as common as a man not wearing pants.

A primitive local government was supported partly by a "Chinaman tax." The tax also applied to persons of Hawaiian or African descent, but there were fewer of them.[3]

Few records survive as to the administration of criminal justice in Jacksonville.

In the spring of 1852, a miner named John Brown, an Illinois Native, shot and killed another miner during a quarrel. Brown said the man had called him a liar, which apparently was not a good enough excuse to murder somebody, even in Jacksonville.

The Sacramento (Calif.) Daily Union of May 24 said Brown was hanged—presumably after a trial of some sort although the newspaper didn't say so.

"We have not been furnished with the name of the deceased," the newspaper added.

Nobody apparently was keeping crime statistics in early Jacksonville, or anywhere else in Oregon for that matter. Only the most sensational incidents had a prayer of being recorded. What little information survives comes from unofficial sources such as newspapers.

Crime of the ordinary kind wasn't southwest Oregon's chief concern in 1825-50, anyway. The entire area between the Siskiyou Mountains on the California border and the headwaters of the Willamette was a battlefield more in need of an Army garrison than a sheriff. Whole groups of combatants had gone to war with one another on a regular basis.

In 1828, Jedediah Smith and seven fellow trappers and their helpers were attacked by Indians on the Umpqua River. Smith escaped but more than a dozen of his party were slain.

Smith was a pioneering mountain-man who had survived more than his share of perils on the frontier. His face was pulled into a perpetual grimace by scars left by a grizzly bear that tore off his scalp and held his head in its jaws. Smith said he promised God he'd pray every day and live a virtuous life from then on, if only the bear would let go of his head. The bear did, and Smith did.

In September, 1837, an outfit returning from California with cattle for the Methodist Mission was attacked by Indians near Foots Creek in present-day Jackson County. The attackers, described as Rogues, an amalgamation of several local tribes, wounded several of the party but lost a dozen of their own.

In May, 1845, John C. Fremont and Kit Carson battled Indians in the Klamath area, losing four of their comrades while killing several attackers and driving off the rest.

Similar conflicts occurred through the 1850s. Gold-seekers traveling to and from California battled frequently with the Natives and with each other.

The perpetual state of warfare slowed settlement of Southwest Oregon for decades.

Portland, wild as it was, had geographic advantages that guaranteed growth, although it shrank at times when a new outbreak of gold fever ripped through the population.

As the biggest city west of St. Louis except for San Francisco, Portland was expected to exercise a civilizing influence but hardly had the means. And neither did the territorial government.

By 1850, Portland was down to just 821 people but was still the only city of consequence in the Pacific Northwest. That gave it the political power to grab the juiciest public works plum the territorial government could offer—a federally-financed penitentiary. There would be lucrative construction contracts to award to the deserving, and cushy jobs to hand out. But considering all the challenges facing Oregon, it may be reasonable to ask why the federal government would prioritize an expensive new building to house convicts.

There was more to it than met the eye.

President Polk believed in Manifest Destiny and wanted to make America's claim to Oregon irreversible by increasing the number of U.S. citizens living there. That meant convincing people back East that Oregon no longer was just a wild and crazy frontier but a reasonable place to relocate and raise a family. If Oregon had anything as civilized as a penitentiary, it would also have public schools and paved streets and churches and a circulating library. A penitentiary also would signal that Oregon was on a par culturally with the most admired states back East.

Reformers in the East were winning the argument that capital punishment not only was unnecessary but could actually make a community less safe by inviting "jury nullification." Nullification was a jury's refusal to return a guilty verdict in a capital case, not because the jury thought the defendant wasn't guilty but because it disapproved of the penalty.

A murder conviction at the time meant a death sentence, almost automatically, which meant a guilty verdict was tantamount to ordering execution.

As penitentiaries became common and offered a credible alternative to capital punishment, jury nullification became less common.

Perhaps surprisingly, not a few judges agreed that juries had a constitutional right to nullify and to apply the law in a way they found consistent with community standards of justice and fairness. Two states, Maryland and Indiana, went so far as to allow judges to instruct juries that they could reject the law itself if they chose.

Some commentators disagreed, saying judicial approval of nullification could "lead to anarchy; that it is unwise or unnecessary (and) better left implicit; or that an instruction on nullification would impair the responsibility of the jurors by confusing them on their duties."

But many juries disagreed with the disagreement and they went on nullifying as they saw fit.[4]

It was only in the later part of the Nineteenth Century that juries were put back on a shorter leash—not to prevent them from sparing defendants but to keep them from inflicting harsher punishments than a judge would allow.

Statistics on nullification were not kept, but the idea of juries as a bulwark against tyranny persists to this day.[5]

Organized movements to abolish the death penalty altogether and make jury nullification unnecessary in capital criminal trials arose as early as the 1790s.

Dr. Benjamin Rush, a Pennsylvania doctor and signer of the Declaration of Independence, was a leading abolitionist. He saw putting people to death as inconsistent with American democracy.

The death penalty, he wrote,

> is the natural offspring of monarchical governments in which kings consider their subjects as their property and no wonder therefore they shed their blood with as little emotion as men shed the blood of their sheep or cattle. But the principles of republican government speak a very different language.[6]

Some of America's capital laws were so random and quirky that they themselves helped make the case for abolition.

Depending on the state, it was punishable by death to kidnap a woman and put her in a harem, to have sex with a lunatic or an imbecile, to commit assault with a deadly weapon while wearing a disguise, or desecrate a grave.

There was never a time in Oregon history that the death penalty wasn't controversial.

President Polk's views on the subject were not widely known, but the priority he placed on building a Territorial penitentiary may tell us something.

Polk's vice president and friend, George M. Dallas, was an outspoken opponent of capital punishment and believed in penitentiaries as an alternative. For a mere vice president, Dallas had unusual political clout. He was a member of one of America's wealthiest and most influential families. His father, the Philadelphia banker Alexander J. Dallas, had been secretary of the treasury under James Madison. George himself was a successful lawyer and a member of the American Philosophical Society, a fraternity of intellectuals founded by Benjamin Franklin. To be elected to membership was a signal honor.

Funding a penitentiary for the new Territory would please Dallas and his cohorts and cost Polk nothing. Local politicians could then be counted upon to think highly of them and President Polk and Democrats generally.

9. NOTES

1. History would be kinder to Meek than Lane. Meek would become a frontier icon on par with Kit Carson or Daniel Boone while Lane would earn lasting disgrace by running on the pro-slavery ticket opposing Abraham Lincoln on the eve of the Civil War.

2. Carolyn Kingsnorth. "Pioneer Profiles: The Fathers of Jacksonville." *Jacksonville Review*, February 2014.

3. Jackson County Records 1853-1920. University of Oregon Libraries, special collections and archives.

4. A. Scheflin, J. Van Dyke. National Criminal Justice Reference Service (NCJRS) *Law and Contemporary Problems*. No. 73179 vol. 43:4. Autumn 1980, pp. 51-115.

5. Article 1, Section 16 of the Oregon Constitution states that, "...in all criminal cases whatever, the jury shall have the right to determine the law, and the facts under the direction of the Court as to the law, and the right of new trial, as in civil cases."

6. National Criminal Justice Reference Service, op.cit.

10.
Portland

Oregon was still a frontier where real money was scarce, and Portland was still a raw, new city where whorehouses and saloons were a significant part of the economy.

Just five years earlier Portland did not even exist, let alone qualify as the location for a penitentiary. The city's principal founder, William Overton, first laid eyes on the place in 1843 when it was nothing but a small clearing in a woods along the Willamette River. Travelers sometimes stopped there to rest on trips between Fort Vancouver and Oregon City.

Overton had just quit his job as a handyman at the Methodist mission at The Dalles and was headed for Oregon City when he overnighted in the clearing as many others had done.

Exploring the land on foot, he found to his surprise that nobody had claimed it. It totaled several hundred acres, and the Willamette River that flowed past was deep and navigable and just a few miles south of where it joined the Columbia.

The possibility of a seaport struck Overton at once. Merchant ships wouldn't have to sail another dozen miles up the Willamette to reach the Provisional capital, Oregon City. With its impassable falls, Oregon City was never suitable as a seaport anyway.

Overton could scarcely believe the site was still there for the taking. The only thing standing between him and owning it was 25 cents. It cost a quarter to file a land claim and Overton didn't have it.

Paddling on up the Willamette to Oregon City he knocked on the door of Asa Lovejoy, a lawyer he'd met at Fort Vancouver. Lovejoy lent him the quarter he needed and handled the paperwork in exchange for half of Overton's claim.

The two men hurried back down the river and posted claim notices and marked off a 16-block city development. They drove stakes in the ground showing future streets and put up signs offering city lots for sale. The claim covered nearly a square mile and the number of potential building sites seemed unlimited.

Lovejoy returned to Oregon City while Overton moved into a log hut beside the river and waited for customers.

Basically, there weren't any.

Overton soon ran out of food and sold Lovejoy another half of his half of the claim for another 25 cents to live on. When that ran out, Overton called it quits.

He traded the remainder of his claim to Lovejoy's partner, Francis W. Pettygrove, for $50 worth of groceries. Then he left for Texas, or some said Tennessee, where he was from. Nobody knew for sure. Overton simply vanished from Oregon history except for a street named after him in Portland's Alphabet Blocks.[1]

With their swindle of Overton complete, Lovejoy and Pettygrove became sole proprietors of a not-yet-existent city. That made them not just Portland's co-founders but arguably its first criminals. Whether they were criminals, or not, depended on whether one used the legal or the moral definition of grand larceny.

In 1845, the two men flipped a one-cent coin for the right to name what they hoped would be a metropolis. Pettygrove won the toss and named it Portland after his hometown in Maine. Lovejoy had hoped to name it Boston.[2]

Choosing a name was the easy part. The "city" they'd founded was mostly primeval forest. The only development for the first year or so was a blacksmith shop with a log shelter next to it for ox teams.

A few brave souls who bought "city lots" had to clear gigantic trees from their property, using bacon grease to lubricate their whipsaws.

Portland grew faster than anyone could have imagined and so did the crime rate. It wasn't long before it approached a scale sufficient to justify what had seemed preposterous: a penitentiary.

The driving force for the rapid change was the gold rush in California. It started in 1848 and set off the fastest Westward migration in U.S. history. It would affect Oregon, too.

An estimated 300,000 to 400,000 Forty-Niners, as they were called, poured into the Golden State in the next three years. To put those numbers into perspective, it had taken 40 years for the first 100,000 people to reach California.

The mad dash for loot sped up nearly everything in the development of the West, including President Polk's decision to send federal troops to Oregon to protect settlers. Many of the troops also caught gold fever.

Brevet Col. William Wing Loring, a one-armed veteran of the Mexican War, lost half his regiment to desertion along the way.

When the Oregon Rifles, as the regiment was known, set out from Fort Leavenworth in the spring of 1849 it had 600 enlisted men, 31 commissioned officers, 61 supply wagons and 200 teamsters to drive them, and dozens of wranglers in charge of 1,700 spare horses and mules, an unspecified number of wives and children and a regimental band.

Food ran short, shoes fell apart, wagons and animals broke down, and wildfires, accidents and illness took a toll. Discipline evaporated and at least 70 troopers made a break for the gold fields when they thought they were close enough.[3]

Several men were caught plotting to kill the regimental paymaster and steal the payroll. What became of them isn't clear.

When Loring's regiment reached Oregon City late that fall, it appeared more in need of help than able to give any. Winter rains were setting in and the men lacked shelter. Local citizens took them in, but they soon wore out their welcome. They drank and did no useful work and brawled and became such a nuisance that many people wished they'd never come.

When spring arrived, 120 deserted as a company and rode south for California. Loring gave chase and caught them near the Umpqua River. He brought 70 back but the rest escaped.

Portland meanwhile was hitting major bumps on the road to cityhood. It had demographics typical of a frontier, with men outnumbering women four to one. The exact count according to the 1850 federal census was 653 to 163. The men were mostly young and single and did what single young men were apt do when left to their own devices. They drank and got into fights and chased women and raised the kind of ruckuses that kept the neighbors from getting a good night's sleep.

Portland clearly had work to do if it wanted to be a real city. It needed a municipal government that could pass ordinances and enforce them. In short, it needed police and courts and a jail.

None of it was going to be easy with so much instability because of gold. But there was an upside: California's population was booming and needed building materials and food in quantities only Oregon could provide.

Oregon wheat and lumber sold for unheard-of prices in the Golden State, but the only practical way to get them to market was by ship. Ships needed seaports and docks and dockworkers and everything else required for the maritime trade.

Portland evolved rapidly from a Northwest version of Deadwood to the bustling port city that Overton had envisioned. By 1850 as many as half a dozen merchant ships could be seen on any given day rocking their masts on the Portland waterfront. Ships from San Francisco brought manufactured goods north and loaded Oregon wheat and lumber for the trip south.

The ships also carried people.

An estimated one-fourth of Oregon's male population left for the California gold fields in 1848-50, some by sea.

And it wasn't just miners doing the traveling. All sorts of people were coming and going, not all of them solid citizens, and Portland morphed rapidly into a port city as wicked as any in the world.

Outlaws, drifters, fugitives, madams, gamblers, and military deserters bumped elbows in Portland's muddy streets with sawmill workers, shopkeepers, lawyers, housewives, schoolteachers, barkeeps, blacksmiths, livery operators, doctors, and ministers of the gospel, plus a special class of fugitives, the ship-jumpers.

Ship-jumpers were merchant seamen who had quit their jobs without permission. It was illegal to do that anywhere in America. Ship-jumpers were treated like runaway slaves.

A man who joined a ship's crew had to sign a contract which bound him to the job. Unlike workers in other trades who could quit if they wanted to, merchant seamen most definitely could not. If they did, they could be arrested and thrown in jail and compelled to go back to work. It was an exception to the constitutional ban on involuntary servitude. Oregon ports were tempting for men desperate to escape and disappear into the countryside.

Gov. Abernethy, who had an interest in the maritime trade, was so vexed by ship-jumpers that he urged the Provisional Legislature in 1846 to punish them severely as a threat to the economy. He also recommended harsh punishment for "any person who shall entice a seaman to leave his ship, or who shall harbor, secrete, employ, or in any wise assist a deserter."

Ship operators, he said, were reluctant to call at Oregon ports because so many crew members went ashore and didn't return. He continued:

> This (enhancement of the ship-jumping law) may appear severe, but when, on reflection, we consider that these men voluntarily entered into a contract to perform certain duties, and that the safety of the vessel they belong to, and the lives and property on board, depend on their faithfully fulfilling

their contract, the severity vanishes at once. We should consider that a vessel lightly manned, (which must be the case if part of the ship's crew desert, as there are no seamen here to supply their places) runs great risks in working out of our harbor—a risk that shipmates and ship-owners will not be likely to run. Unless regulations be made that will prevent desertion, owners of vessels will avoid our ports, and without vessels, the produce of the farmer must remain on his hands, and in this way work an injury all round, and one that will be felt by all classes in the community.[4]

Abernethy neglected to mention his personal stake in the legislation. His store made money re-provisioning ships.

The Assembly declined to act on the governor's request except to require ship operators to post bond guaranteeing to hunt down and remove any Black seaman who deserted.

A Black seaman might have had special reason to desert in Oregon, but there was no mystery as to why any seaman of any color would want to quit. The job was downright medieval.

A ship captain practically owned his men. They had no rights to speak of, and working conditions at sea were often brutal. A captain could have a man flogged for any reason that struck his fancy. A merchant ship was like a floating penal colony.

The U.S. Supreme Court thought this whole arrangement, built around un-quitable jobs, was perfectly acceptable.

As late as 1897 it upheld the constitutionality of seamens' contracts in an Oregon case brought by four crew members who jumped ship in Astoria. The men were arrested by the U.S. marshal and appealed to the Court, which promptly ruled against them. The Thirteenth Amendment prohibiting involuntary servitude, didn't apply to them, the Court said, accepting the usual argument that they waived that right when they signed on.

The rebellious seamen were Robert Robertson, P. H. Olsen, John Bradley and Morris Hansen.

When they refused to rejoin their ship, the marshal forced them back aboard. They still refused to work and were jailed again when they got to San Francisco.[5]

Not only did many men serve at sea against their will but more than a few were tricked or coerced into doing so by waterfront racketeers known as "crimps." Portland was home to two of the most notorious on the West Coast—Bunko Kelly and Jim Turk.

Turk was a barroom brawler and slumlord who used his flophouses as trap. If a naive young man needed a place to sleep, Turk would give him a bed on credit and wait for him to rack up a bill he couldn't pay and then march him down to a ship and force him to sign on. The captain would pay Turk a finder's fee plus whatever back-rent his victim owed. Later the captain would recoup the money by taking it out of the victim's wages.[6]

Portland's bad reputation wasn't just because of crimps but for something even worse, shanghai artists.

Shanghai artists were kidnapers who delivered men to ships without even a pretense of consent. They were usually crimps, as well, so they used whichever method was convenient. They generally got their victims on board by first getting them blind-drunk or slipping them a "mickey"—a knockout drug—to neutralize resistance.

Bunko Kelly claimed he victimized not just prospective crewmen but also ship captains, on occasion, with ruses so outrageous as to beggar belief. Once, he claimed, he sold a captain a cigar store Indian wrapped in a blanket. And on another occasion, he said, he sold a captain 22 dead men.

Since shanghai victims usually were carried aboard unconscious or nearly so, Kelly said the captain accepted his story that the men were just drunk and sleeping it off. In fact, he said, they'd killed themselves drinking embalming fluid in a mortuary basement they mistook for a distillery.

Whether it was possible for even the most dedicated drunk to mistake embalming fluid for liquor was a good question.

But Kelly insisted the story was true and that the captain paid him $52 per corpse and was well at sea before discovering he'd been swindled.

Kelly was never convicted of shanghaiing but later in life served 13 years in Oregon State Penitentiary for murder. He wrote a book about it later.[7]

10. NOTES

1. Carl Abbott. *Portland in Three Centuries: The Place and the People.* Oregon State University Press, Corvallis OR 2022, pp. 20-22.

2. Carl Abbott. *Portland: Gateway to the Northwest.* Windsor Publications, Inc., Northridge CA 1985, pp. 17-19.

3. Frances Fuller Victor. "The First Oregon Cavalry." *Oregon Historical Quarterly*, vol. 3, 1902.

4. "Journals, Governors' Messages and Public Papers of Oregon. Dec. 1, 1846." Oregon Archives. Asahel Bush, Public Printer. Salem OR 1853.

5. *Robertson v. Baldwin,* 165 U.S. 275 (1897). Library of Congress. Also, Blackstone's *Commentaries on the Laws of England,* Volume 1, p. 134.

6. Finn John. *Wicked Portland: The Wild and Lusty Underworld of a Frontier Seaport Town.* The History Press. 2012.

7. (Joseph) Bunko Kelly. *Thirteen Years in the Oregon Penitentiary.* Portland OR. 1908. Published privately for Kelly.

11.
Ordinary crimes

Most of Portland's lawbreaking didn't involve niche crimes like crimping and shanghaiing, but the ordinary kind. Larceny and assault were mostly what kept the courts busy.

Men returning from the gold fields with money in their pockets found plenty of ways to spend it and plenty of new friends to help them. Portland's saloons did double-duty as gambling dens that took a cut from card sharps and other cheats they allowed to operate.

Even Oregon City, the former Methodist Mission stronghold, lost its virtue.

"It was hardly safe to be in the streets late at night," a citizen named Miller was quoted in the Oregon City newspaper. Miller went on:

> One man was murdered. Games of all kinds and descriptions that could be played with cards were going (on) and thousands of dollars-worth of gold dust were on the gaming tables. It seemed that those who were lucky in the mines and who made a fortune, handled their dust lavishly, bet it by the ounce on a single card at Monte, or on a hand of cards at poker, or any other game. They seem to feel that if they lost all they had, all they would have to do would be to go to California and dig up another sack full of gold. Everybody was too rich or too lazy to work.

Over the long haul, what caused the great majority of Americans to move West wasn't gold or adventure but free public land.

Congress passed the Oregon Donation Land Law in September 1850, allowing white male Americans to claim 320 acres—half a square mile—if they occupied and worked it for at least four years. Half-Indian men also could file a claim—a nod to the numerous "fur-trade marriages" between white men and Indian women during the Hudson's Bay era. Their offspring made up a significant part of the population.

However, full-blooded Native American men whose ancestors had lived in Oregon for thousands of years were not allowed to file claims. Nor were Blacks or Kanakas (Hawaiians) or anyone, regardless of race, who was not an American citizen.

Single women also were ineligible. But if a woman was married, she and her husband could claim a full section, 640 acres. One square mile. That provided instant wealth for couples and an incentive for singles to defraud the United States.

With adult single women very scarce on the frontier, barely-pubescent girls could be a valuable commodity. Girls as young as 12 were allowed to marry under common law, with parental consent, so parents lucky enough to have a marriageable girl had a marketable item. A marriage to which they consented might be "real" or might exist just long enough for the ink to dry on a land claim. It's not hard to imagine deals being struck and money changing hands.

The Donation Land law did do what it was supposed to do, however, and helped populate the West faster than might have happened otherwise. The downside was that the large size of claims kept settlement sparse and slowed the development of non-agricultural sectors of the economy.[1]

Free land also accelerated the displacement of indigenous peoples by settlers who saw the country as empty and there for the taking. But it wasn't empty. It was somebody's home and had been so for a long time.

When Maj. Gen. John E. Wool took command of the U.S. Army garrison in Oregon in 1853, he asked the War Department for more troops—not to protect whites from the Indians but to "protect the Indians against the white men."[2]

As time went on, the Native peoples weren't the only ones to suffer discrimination.

Ethnic Chinese in Oregon had to pay a special tax, essentially for being Chinese. The early government was financed mostly from fees on occupational or business licenses. People of Chinese descent were charged double what everyone else had to pay. A one-dollar gold-mining license cost two dollars if you made the mistake of being Chinese.

Oregon's "Chinaman tax" applied not just to gold-mining licenses but also to "trading, selling or buying goods, chattels or any property whatever for the purpose of maintaining a livelihood."[3]

Obviously a fully-functioning government couldn't run just on license fees even if Chinese residents were charged double. So, Polk's gift of federal funds to build a penitentiary became a prize worth fighting over.

The battle began early in 1850 when the Territorial Legislature tried to withdraw $20,000 from the fund to start construction and spread a little of that money around. Gov. John P. Gaines, a conservative Whig, professed outrage that the Democrat-controlled Legislature had acted without consulting him, so he refused to recognize the appropriation as lawful.

Meanwhile, it dawned on the Legislature that it had awarded the penitentiary to a city that did not yet legally exist. It corrected that minor oversight on Jan. 14, 1851 by issuing Portland a city charter.

A city election was held in April and Hugh D. O'Bryant, a Georgia transplant who ran a general store in Oregon City, was chosen mayor. Five Portland businessmen were elected to the city council, all but one of whom had dealings with the city that wouldn't pass the smell test today.[4]

When the councilmen weren't selling things to the city, such as candlesticks to illuminate council meetings, or rent for a room they used, they addressed crime.

Portland City Ordinance No. 1 authorized hiring a "competent and discreet person to act as city marshal."

It took seven contentious ballots but the council on April 14, 1851 chose New York native Hiram Wilbur.

Wilbur, a "quiet man of high repute" came west with John C. Fremont on some kind of railroad survey. Wilbur had no apparent police experience, and with that, he waded into the wide-open city of Portland where many people carried guns.[5]

Just days before Wilbur took the job, a gambler named William Kean (or Keene) shot and killed William Cook, not otherwise identified, in front of a saloon on Front Street. Wilbur arrested Kean and locked him up to await trial. As Portland didn't have a jail, it's not clear where that was. Washington County, which then included Portland, had just spent $900 on a small wooden structure that looked more like a henhouse. That may be where Kean was kept.

Kean got a quick trial and a manslaughter conviction, drawing a six-month sentence. Where he did the six months is hard to say unless it was the henhouse.

Shortly after the Cook murder, William Kendall, a Marion County farmer, killed a neighbor in a dispute over hogs. Kendall was sentenced to hang, but as the county had no jail to keep him while he waited, he was put in irons and boarded with a family named Munker.

Counting the cost of room and board and a tavern bill for a last meal, plus the sheriff's fee for doing the hanging, the taxpayers were out $1,951 for disposing of farmer Kendall.

Wilbur had to wonder right away if the job he'd taken was worth it. He didn't get a regular paycheck but had to bill the city for each service he performed. He got a certain amount for appearing in court, a certain amount for lighting streetlamps, a certain amount for collecting city taxes, and so on. He was also the dog-catcher and health officer.

As health officer, Wilbur had to knock on doors and tell property owners to clean up trash "or filth of any kind whatever."

If he ran across anyone with smallpox he was supposed to take him, or her, to the city "pest house" to be quarantined. If he failed to do so, he could be fined.

There are no surviving records of a pest house or where it was located if it ever actually existed.

Wilbur also had to enforce miscellaneous city ordinances such as one making it illegal to "discharge any firearm within the limits of the city" or to drive a horse or wagon through the streets "at a furious pace."

Public drunkenness also was prohibited as was "rioting or in any way disturbing the peace."

Being city marshal was a 24/7 job and Wilbur was a one-man department.

The council didn't make it clear as to what, exactly, Wilbur was supposed to do about things that weren't necessarily crimes but were highly annoying.

An old cannon had been installed on the city docks to be fired whenever a merchant ship appeared on the river, and now and then some prankster would set it off in the middle of the night, greatly vexing the townfolk who demanded the marshal do something.

Whether Wilbur had to claim a fee every time he arrested an alleged criminal or dealt with a prankster is unclear.

As there was no city jail, violations of city ordinances were punished mostly by a $10 fine. It was not a trivial amount at that time, when a dozen eggs cost a dime and a live turkey could be bought for 30 cents.

Wilbur served about three months and quit. By 1863 he appeared to have left Oregon altogether. His replacement was William L. Higgins, a craggy-faced Rhode Island seaman and ship's carpenter who'd lost only narrowly to Wilbur in the first vote to select a marshal.

Higgins took over on June 4, 1851 and served nearly two years.

One of his first jobs was investigating the love-triangle murder of Edward Bradbury, the 24-year-old son of a wealthy Ohio seed oil manufacturer.

Bradbury had just moved into a boarding house on the outskirts of Portland in October 1851 when he was stabbed to death.

His killer, Creed Turner, was already living there. Turner was 29 years old and had been romancing 14-year-old Martha Jane Bonser whose parents ran the boarding house.

Bradbury started flirting with her, too, sending Turner into a jealous rage. As the boarders sat at dinner one evening, Turner drew a dagger and walked around the table and stabbed Bradbury repeatedly, killing him.

Although the boarding house was outside Portland's city limit, Higgins investigated and arrested Turner on the spot. A jury on November 4 convicted him of murder after a one-day trial and he was sentenced to hang.

On the eve of his execution, according to a newspaper account, Turner ate a last meal and had a shave and asked to be baptized, but arrangements couldn't be made in time. Visitors said they heard Turner muttering to himself frantically as he tried to finish writing what he called his autobiography.[6]

Dressed in the shroud he'd be buried in, Turner climbed the steps of the gallows and stood on the trap door as the noose was adjusted. His hangman was Sheriff William Hardin Bennett, 25, a Kentucky native.

Turner had only a moment to look out on a crowd of about 250 before the trap door opened and he dropped through. He died instantly of a broken neck but was allowed to dangle for about 20 minutes to satisfy the crowd. Then his body was taken down and placed in a pine box provided by the county and buried in an unmarked grave.

Higgins was Portland's last appointed marshal.

The job was made elective and the first to win at the ballot box was a frizzy-bearded Englishman named Thomas J. Holmes, a printer by trade, who'd just arrived from San Francisco.

After his election, he persuaded the city council to let him hire eight night guards to protect the city in case of Indian attack.

When no Indians appeared, Holmes had to lay off the guards and busy himself going after Portland's vice dens. That won him the approval of Thomas J. Dryer, publisher and editor of The Weekly Oregonian whose favorite whipping-boys were the city's "drunkards, dope fiends and jack-leg gamblers."

Holmes basked in Dryer's editorial approval until he got caught taking bribes and was thrown out of office.

Former marshal Higgins replaced him.

During his prior tour of duty, Higgins' signature achievement had been persuading the city council to build a jail. The council bought two lots for $130 on the east side of 6th Avenue between Alder and Washington streets and hired Ira Ward, a contractor, to put up a building.

The result, essentially, was a big one-room cabin made of hewn timber, measuring 16x25 feet. It had a single door with a lock and no documented creature comforts other than a roof. The marshal used part of the jail as his office.[7]

How prisoners were supposed to sleep, eat or relieve themselves wasn't clear.

And there was another problem: When the marshal locked up and went home at night, friends of the inmates sometimes broke in and freed them.

The only remedy was to have a guard there all the time.

The council now realized that the real cost of having a jail was less about the cost of building than the cost of running it. A 24-hour guard was expensive, and taxes were just as unpopular then as now.

The council found a way out by unloading the jail on the Territorial government as a temporary "penitentiary" until the real one could be built.

The council needn't have worried about operating costs, however, as the jail soon burned to the ground. The council then billed the Territory for loss of the building because it had happened under Territorial control.

With the jail/penitentiary in ashes, prisoners were locked in a vacant whiskey shop on Front Street owned by William M. King, a prominent Portland businessman and politician. In the words of historian Malcolm Clark Jr., King was "distinguished by an illuminated nose and a conniving nature."[8]

Before moving to Oregon from Pennsylvania, King had been a construction contractor on the Erie Canal and "appreciated the profits to be made from suitably handled public works," according to Clark.

On Feb. 1, 1851, King got a chance to get into the penitentiary business in a big way. The Territorial Legislature appointed him to lead a three-man board of commissioners to oversee construction and how a lot of money got spent. King just happened to be Speaker of the House at the time, which did not harm his chances for getting the appointment.

The penitentiary would be the biggest and most expensive public works project west of the Mississippi. It would be 100 percent federally-funded—"free money" as far as Oregonians were concerned, requiring no disagreeable new taxes and less scrutiny of expenditures. The only strenuous labor required of Oregon officials would be signing requisitions for cash from the fund President Polk had sent.

An architect's concept drawing of the penitentiary showed a multi-story Roman-revival edifice topped by a cupola, with a colonnaded entry of impressive size, making it look less like an abode for convicts than the capital of some medium-size country.

Specifications required that the building be of sufficient size "to receive, secure and employ 100 convicts to be confined in separate cells at night."

It was a far cry from how convicts sometimes were kept in the pioneer Northwest. In two known instances, prisoners were housed in holes in the ground. An aggressive drunk called "the Bad Swede" had so frightened the inhabitants of a Montana mining camp that he was put down a 30-foot prospect hole to serve his time. Food and drink were lowered on a string. When his time was up, a rope was put down and he was allowed to climb out.

Criminal trials also were seat-of-the-pants affairs.

John J. McGilvra, the first U.S. attorney for the Washington Territory when it was split off from Oregon, recalled court being held in the attic of a log saloon with no interruption of the drinking and card-playing going on below. The judge's bench was a wash stand, and spectators sat on log slabs supported by peg legs, and defendants were chained to the wall.

One judge who traveled a circuit had to hold court in a settler's cabin when no other building was available due to the lateness of the hour. The judge and his retinue, including a sheriff and a captured outlaw, barged into the cabin and found the settler in bed asleep.

"We're going to hold court," the judge announced to the startled occupant who complained, and kept complaining, about having his rest disturbed.

"Five dollars for contempt of court," the judge rapped his gavel.

"Court?" the settler said. "I didn't know you had a court here."

"Joe," replied the judge, "I want you to understand that wherever I take off my hat the court is in session."[9]

Against this backdrop, the idea of Oregon building a modern penitentiary may have seemed premature.

But King and his co-commissioners were ordered to get things moving, which they did, only to hit a snag. The legislation that authorized them to select a building site did not authorize them to buy it. So, nothing was done for almost two years.

The difficulty early in the process was political feuding between the conservative governor and the Democratic Legislature. It wasn't until 1853 that the politicians got out of their own way and a new board was appointed and authorized to buy land and put a building on it.

But there was yet another problem: Expensive design changes. The Territorial government now decided that the penitentiary should be large enough to hold 150 prisoners instead of the 100 originally planned. And it had to be built of brick and stone, much costlier than wood which Oregon had in abundance, but was not fireproof.

King's new partners on the board of commissioners were Samuel Parker, a member of the Provisional Legislature, and Nathaniel Ford, a sourpuss ex-sheriff who had brought his three slaves along when he immigrated from Missouri.

The new board bought two city blocks as a building site on Southwest Front Street between Hall and Harrison near the Willamette River, paying $1,200 for the pair.

The combined lots were big enough for the 114x50 foot building the government now wanted. It would contain three tiers of cells, 26 cells per tier, for a total of 78. The floors and interior walls would be stone.

The cells would be stacked back-to-back in rows in the middle of the building, accessible by catwalks. Each cell would have a solid iron door with a peep-hole like a mail slot, allowing prisoners a narrow view of the outer walls and their long, barred windows.

But if the prison was filled to 150-inmate capacity, more than one man would have to be housed in nearly all the cells. It was a major departure from the original specification calling for one man per cell.

And there was an even bigger issue: The two lots the commissioners bought were on opposite sides of Front Street, and the City of Portland refused to vacate the street. Why this wasn't straightened out before the commissioners bought the lots is a good question.

King's part in the fiasco and his prominence as a Democrat assured that he'd be skewered by his political enemies, chiefly editor Dryer of The Weekly Oregonian.

Dryer lampooned King as a drunken incompetent, and King didn't help himself by making some poor decisions. Because penitentiary construction was plagued by delays, he rented a vacant whiskey shop to the Territory as a temporary prison until the real one could be built.

King owned the shop and it was never meant to hold prisoners, and, big surprise, it didn't. The escape rate was approximately 100 percent.

"We understand," wrote Dryer, "that Sellers who was recently convicted in Marion County of robbing the store of Schlussel & Cohen and sentenced to the penitentiary has escaped from custody. And the Indian who was convicted of stealing horses has left again. These, the only two persons sentenced have taken French leave of their keeper."

King's repeated missteps kept Dryer busy inventing new ways to ridicule him.

> On the evening which the convicts made their escape we are informed that they gave Shakespearean recitations with their shackles off that they might gesticulate more freely. Their limbs being thus at liberty and the stomachs of their keepers being well plied with whiskey, they made an easy escape. Such is the character of those who have charge of the convicts. How long will it be that the people of Oregon must submit to such a state of things as are being practiced upon them at public expense.

When the whiskey store burned down—something of a tradition for Oregon jails—Dryer made a fresh attack on King.

"The commissioner and his humbug keeper," he wrote, "will have plenty of time to make out the report to the Legislature which is to meet in a few days."

But the Legislature didn't wait. It fired King and his fellow commissioners and replaced them with three new ones: Dr. William S. Ladd, a former Portland mayor; C. W. Fitch, a lawyer lately of Pennsylvania; and a man named Belknap.[10]

With the City refusing to budge on the street vacation request, the new commissioners rented a farmhouse at a different location on Front between Miller and Montgomery to use as a temporary prison. The owner-occupant, F. M. Arnold, was made assistant keeper and paid three dollars a day per convict for salary and expenses.

Not much is known about Arnold, but his photograph showed a large, robust man with a neatly-trimmed beard, wearing a business suit with a masonic pin prominent on one lapel.

During the Arnold era, more design changes hampered progress on the penitentiary while crime continued apace.

11. NOTES

1. See Johansen's *Empire of the Columbia,* op. cit.

2. F. G. Young. "Financial History of Oregon Part Two, Finances of the Territorial Period, 1849-1859." *Oregon Historical Quarterly*, vol. 8, 1907, pp. 129-190.

3. Ibid.

4. *Transactions of the Annual Reunion of the Oregon Pioneer Association,* vol. 46. 1918.

5. Jim Huff. *Portland Police to 1870.* Portland Police Museum and Historical Society. https://www.portlandpolicemuseum.com/s/stories/portland-police-to-1870; Also, Letter to the Editor, The Oregon Daily Journal. Sept. 27, 1953.

6. Diane L. Goeres-Gardner. *Necktie Parties*. Caxton Press, Caldwell ID 2005.

7. Portland City Archives, file AD/22569.

8. Malcolm Clark, Jr. *Eden Seekers - The Settlement of Oregon, 1818-1862.* Houghton Mifflin Company. Boston 1981, p. 245.

9. William J. Airey. *A History of the Constitution and Government of Washington Territory.* PhD thesis, University of Washington, 1945. p. 311. Also, *Oregon Historical Quarterly*, vol. 61, 1960, pp. 294-95.

10. King's connection with the penitentiary wasn't quite over, however, He and a business partner, George Kittredge, would be investigated later for selling supplies to the contractor who built and initially operated the penitentiary.

12.
Wit's end

Exactly how much crime was committed in penitentiary-free Oregon is impossible to say since nobody was keeping track. It's fairly certain, however, that perpetrators were almost all male, because women rarely committed crime and especially not murder.

There was, however, a famous exception: Charity Lamb.[1]

Charity and her husband, Nathaniel, hailed originally from North Carolina and lived briefly in Missouri before migrating to Oregon with their four children. They homesteaded a 318-acre farm ten miles up the Clackamas River from Oregon City where they lived quietly until Saturday, May 13, 1854, when Charity struck her husband twice in the head with an axe as he sat at the dinner table. Then she went to a neighbor's cabin a half mile away where a constable found her smoking a pipe.

"I did not mean to kill the critter," she told the constable, "I only meant to stun him."

Nathaniel lingered for a week before dying.

Rumors spread that Charity and her 17-year-old daughter, Mary Ann, had been carrying on with a drifter named Collins and planned to flee with him to California. Mary Ann was indicted for murder along with her mother, but was acquitted after a trial lasting less than a day. The rumors were easily proved false.

Charity meanwhile was kept in jail to await a September trial in the U.S. District Court in Oregon City. The Oregonian said she walked into the courtroom looking pale and emaciated, with an infant in arms. She pleaded not guilty although she had made numerous public admissions already.

Her defense lawyer argued that Charity had acted on a well-founded fear of being murdered by her husband and killed him in self-defense.

Witnesses supported her claim.

Two of her children, Mary Ann, 19, and Abram, 13, testified that their father kicked and beat their mother with his fists on numerous occasions. They said he struck her with a hammer and pointed a gun at her and threatened repeatedly to kill her.

Only men were allowed to serve on juries, and a jury of 12 men convicted Charity of second-degree murder. They said there wasn't a close enough nexus between the abuse and her striking him with an axe to call it self-defense. They did ask the judge to show leniency, but the judge explained that a life sentence was mandatory under the law.

He told Charity that the jury thought she should have run away if she felt threatened. But Charity said she hadn't dared, that her husband vowed to track her down and shoot her if she did. "And he was a mighty good shot," she said.

After Charity was sentenced, her baby was taken away from her and she spent the next two years in a local jail. Her minor children were sent to other people to raise, and the family farm was auctioned off to pay their expenses.

Where, exactly, Charity was supposed to serve a life sentence wasn't clear. The penitentiary was still under construction and little thought apparently had been given to the possibility of female prisoners.

When the building was close to completion in July 1857, she and 17 male prisoners were escorted inside and locked in temporary wooden cells.

Superintendent Joseph Sloan, first to occupy that position, put Charity to work doing laundry. At first it was just laundry for him and his family and for other inmates. But as time went on, she was seen around town picking up laundry from people with no connection to the prison. What she earned and what became of the money is unknown.

Charity obviously had many opportunities to escape while moving around town without an escort, but she never tried.

An effort was made in 1860 to have her pardoned but it failed.

In 1862, she was transferred to a new insane asylum in east Portland owned and operated by Drs. James C. Hawthorne and A.M. Loryea. It was near 12th Avenue on what is now Hawthorne Boulevard. The State of Oregon—Oregon by now was a state—had contracted with Dr. Hawthorne and Dr. Loryea to provide asylum services for "indigent insane and idiotic persons" committed by the courts.

A grandson of Charity's said later that she was neither insane nor mentally impaired, but was transferred to the asylum for humanitarian reasons.

By 1863, she was one of 34 residents, five of whom were women.

State inspectors who visited the Hawthorne asylum in 1865 noted that Charity "sat knitting as the visiting party went through the hall, face imperturbably fixed in half-smiling contentment apparently as satisfied with her lot as the happiest of sane people with theirs."[2]

Charity Lamb died in 1879, reportedly of a stroke, and was buried with more than 100 other deceased and unclaimed patients in a corner of Lone Fir Cemetery in Southeast Portland.[3]

For a close-up description of crime and punishment in Oregon in the mid-1800s, there may be no better witness than Martha Gilliam Collins.

She arrived in the Territory with her parents in 1843 and sat down years later for an extended interview with Fred Lockley, editor of The Oregon Journal.[4]

Lockley liked to gather oral histories from pioneers, and here are some highlights of what she told him.

> In February, 1852, William Everman killed Seranas C. Hooker, a Polk County farmer. Hooker accused Everman of stealing his watch. My brother had the unpleasant duty of hanging Everman.
>
> Everman's brother, Hiram, was arrested as an accomplice. He had helped his brother get away. Hiram was generally considered a good man. I believe that William Everman, who killed Hooker, was mentally unbalanced. Enoch Smith was sentenced to be hung for being an accessory to the crime, but was pardoned and David Coe, who was also tried for being an accomplice, secured a change of venue and was acquitted.
>
> Hiram was sentenced to three years in the penitentiary but as there was no penitentiary and they didn't want to build one for the exclusive benefit of Hiram Everman, they decided to sell him at auction. Dave Grant, who was a brother-in-law of Sheriff Smith Gilliam, was the auctioneer. They put him up for sale in Dallas (Oregon, near Salem).
>
> Hiram was sold the day his brother was hung. Theodore Prather bought him. When he had worked out his three years Prather gave him a horse and saddle and twenty dollars. He went to Douglas County and raised a family and was a good citizen.
>
> Frank Nichols, who married my sister Sarah, was the next sheriff. One of his first jobs was hanging Adam E. Wimple. Wimple had stayed for a while at our house in 1845. He married a 13-year-old girl in 1850 and within a year killed her.
>
> They lived in Cooper Hollow, four or five miles from Dallas. My brother-in-law, Alec Gage, and his wife stopped at Wimple's house the morning he killed her. Mrs. Wimple's face was all swollen and her eyes were red from crying. Wimple saw they noticed it, so he said 'Mary isn't feeling very well this morning.' My brother-in-law and his wife had not gone over a mile and a half when they saw smoke rising from where the Wimple house was. They hurried back and found the house in flames. It was too late to save anything in the house. When the fire had burned out they found

Mrs. Wimple under the floor partially burned. Wimple had disappeared. He was more than double her age. She was 14 and he was about 35. A posse captured him and brought him to Dallas. I knew Wimple well, so I asked him why he had killed Mary. He said, 'Well, I killed her. I don't really know why.

Collins said she thought Wimple might have been insane.

There was no jail, so Frank Nichols took Wimple to his house to stay. Frank swore in four guards, but Wimple got away and was gone four days before they found him and brought him back. They tracked him to the house where he had killed his wife. I went over to stay with my sister, Mrs. Nichols, while he was boarding there waiting to be hung and I helped her cook for him. Frank hung him early in October, 1852. Wimple sat on his coffin in the wagon when they drove to the gallows where he was to be hung. They passed the sheriff's father, Uncle Ben Nichols, while they were on their way to the gallows. Wimple was afraid Uncle Ben would be late and miss the hanging, so he called out 'Uncle Ben, ain't you going to the hanging? Ain't you coming down to see me hung?' Uncle Ben said, 'I have seen enough of you, Adam. No, I ain't going.' Uncle Ben was the only man in Polk County to receive a personal invitation and he was about the only one who didn't take a day off to see the hanging.

In her interview, Collins mentioned insanity several times and not always in connection with crime.

The Oregon Provisional Assembly in 1845 set aside $200 for the care of "lunatics," a surprisingly measly sum considering the number of people who might be expected to fit that description. The money was used to compensate private caretakers as Oregon had no insane asylum.

Collins told Lockley she doubted the sanity of several murderers with whom she was acquainted including one or two who were considered too dangerous to board out while awaiting trial.

Oregon did not yet allow an insanity defense for murder but it was beginning to catch on in the East. The impetus was a landmark ruling in Great Britain in 1843, called the M'Naghten rule.

An English judge decided that Daniel M'Naghten, a woodcutter, was insane and therefore not guilty when he shot and killed Edward Drummond, Prime Minister Robert Peel's secretary. The defense spread to the United States in 1847 and found its way to Oregon.

Although statistics weren't kept, any number of Oregonians likely could have beaten the hangman at that time by invoking the M'Naghten rule. Not all "lunatics" were criminals, of course, but people sometimes did go crazy enough to be mentioned in letters home.

Asa Munger, a carpenter at the Whitman Mission on the Upper Columbia, had a spectacular breakdown in 1841, under the delusion that he was a prophet and lawgiver like Moses and had to be obeyed.

"Our Brother Munger is perfectly insane and we are tried to know how to get along with him," Narcissa Whitman wrote to a friend.

At their wits' end, the Whitmans sent Munger and his wife to Oregon City in hopes they could be put on a ship and sent home to relatives.

But it was too late.

"After driving two nails in his left hand," Narcissa wrote to her sister, "Brother Munger drew out a bed of hot coals and laid himself down upon it, thrusting his hand into the hottest part of the fire and burnt it to a crisp, and he died four days later."

Munger's widow never returned East. She married a farmer and lived out her life in the Puget Sound area.

Laws to care for the insane had been among the first enacted by the Provisional government when it organized itself in 1843.

As there was no asylum, the law required the county sheriff to summon "a jury of twelve intelligent and impartial men" to investigate whether a person was truly mad. If the answer was yes, guardians were appointed to sell the person's property and use the proceeds to pay for care. A Probate Court supervised.

If the insane person had no property, the guardians were obliged to use their own resources to ensure that the "unfortunates" received "relief as paupers and maintained under the care of the Overseers of the Poor."

The guardians also had to arrange care for the insane person's family.

If the guardians didn't have enough money to carry out their assignment, the county had to pay. This led to quarreling between counties as to which one was responsible, and sometimes between counties and the central government. With money definitely an issue, a law was soon passed requiring that insane persons be "let out publicly… to the lowest bidder, to be boarded and clothed for one year…"

Five "lunatics" were so identified in 1850 out of a population of 13,294.

But the tussle over financial responsibility continued.

The law that let counties apply for Territorial insanity funds was repealed in 1856 and the counties had to shift for themselves.[6]

As the mid-Nineteenth Century rolled on, Editor Dryer stopped harping about Portland's shortcomings and took on the unfamiliar role of civic booster-in-chief. The city's businessmen, who were also Dryer's advertisers, convinced him there was much more to be gained by bragging about the city than cussing it. The 1855 provisional census, Dryer reported, showed that Portland had:

> four churches, an academy, a public school, one steam flour mill, four steam saw mills, four printing offices, two express offices, four doctors' and six lawyers' offices, two dentists, five cabinet shops, three bakeries, four stove and tin stores, two tailoring establishments, two jewelers, four blacksmithing shops, one foundry, three wagon makers, six painters, two boat builders, six livery stables, twelve hotels and boarding houses, three butchers, six saloons, two bowling alleys, one book store, one drug store, one Daguerrean gallery, one shoe store, one candy manufactory, and several cigar stores.

Besides the foregoing, he said, "there were twenty-five establishments dealing in dry goods, groceries, &c., together with ten establishments engaged exclusively in dry goods, and seven in groceries only."

The census didn't enumerate Portland's bordellos and gambling joints but they may have been lumped in with boarding houses, hotels and saloons.

Also omitted was any mention of the penitentiary or another of the city's hard-to-miss features: tree stumps in the streets. They were big and they had to be whitewashed for traffic safety until they could be removed.

"Stumptown" was a nickname that stuck.

Early in 1854, authorities started sending prisoners to the penitentiary even though it was still under construction. Three were put in unfinished cells and one immediately escaped, leaving two. Six more were received and three escaped, leaving five. Two of the five died of unspecified causes, leaving three.

Lack of funds hampered further progress on construction for the next few years including what to do about the prison's leaky flagstone floors. They were un-grouted, and when the floors on the upper tiers were mopped, water ran down through cracks and showered everybody on the tiers below.

Meanwhile, local law enforcement was undergoing major change. Multnomah County was carved out of Washington and Clackamas counties and Portland suddenly was the seat of a county with no sheriff or jail.

When Multnomah County's inaugural board of commissioners met for the first time Jan. 17, 1855, its first official act was to appoint a sheriff. It pinned the badge on William L. McMillen, a stout millwright from Oregon City.

McMillen had been working at Abernethy's flour mill and was a militant teetotaler like his boss. At Abernethy's behest, but without any legal authority whatsoever, McMillen had traveled to Astoria and destroyed a liquor store and arrested the owner at gunpoint.

Not much is known about McMillen's doings as Multnomah County's first sheriff, but it's easy to guess he enforced liquor laws to the hilt.[7]

Meanwhile, Portland city voters elected William B. Grooms, a native of Kingston, Canada, as their new city marshal. The job continued to be paid by piecework rather than by salary, and the results were unsatisfactory, according to Editor Dryer.

The marshal, he complained, did little of any use while the city suffered from bands of "vagabonds hanging around the low groggeries in the daytime and destroying property at night." Dryer suggested forming an "armed vigilance committee" to restore order but got no takers.

Seven city marshals came and went during the 1850s. Sometimes it was hard to tell the lawmen from the outlaws because they might be the same people.

"Any desperado who had the necessary abilities could always get himself elected city marshal," wrote Edouard "Frenchy" Chambreau in an 1870 memoir.[8]

Chambreau knew all about scamming his way into a law enforcement job. He was a career criminal himself and part-owner at one time of the Oro Fino, Portland's pre-eminent saloon and vice den. His partner was James Lappeus, a professional crook of long standing and low repute. Lappeus ran successfully for city marshal in 1859 and lasted about a year before he was caught soliciting bribes. The last straw was offering to let a murderer escape from jail if his family could come up with $1,000.

Lappeus and Chambreau worked together to make sure dissatisfied customers at Oro Fino got no help from the police. However, the police did find time to arrest a few temperance advocates for singing hymns outside the saloon, charging them with disturbing the peace.[9]

Portland's marshal system lasted until 1870 when the city created a modern police department. The first chief, who was also the last city marshal, was Phillip Saunders, a 41-year-old native of County Cork, Ireland. Saunders wasn't corrupt, but took to the bottle and died in the new state insane asylum in Salem.[10]

When Oregon became a state in 1859 it tried a new way to manage the penitentiary—leasing it to private contractors. The first were Robert "Doc" Newell, a grizzled former fur trapper who'd helped form Oregon's provisional government, and a partner, L. N. English, a well-to-do farmer from Illinois.

English had a reputation as an innovator and it may have been his idea to turn the penitentiary into a business. The convicts would be put to work and a profit would be made on their labor. Just what kind of labor wasn't clear. But it didn't matter. All the convicts escaped before the plan could be tried. The state cancelled the contract and returned to conventional management.

Alva Compton Riggs Shaw, better known as A.C.R. Shaw—would be the last superintendent of the penitentiary at the Portland location. Then he'd be the first when it was moved to Salem.

Shaw was appointed by Gov. A. C. Gibbs in 1862 and served four years. Why Gibbs chose him is a good question, as Shaw had no qualifications that anyone knew of for running a prison. He was a New Yorker who'd helped his stepfather drive a herd of sheep from Illinois to Oregon in 1844. He was still in the sheep business when he got the superintendent job.

As the last official to hold that job in Portland, Shaw tried making the prison pay for itself by putting the inmates to work making saddles and related equipment.

Hoping to attract customers who may have had doubts about convict craftsmanship, Shaw tacked up handbills around town saying "that the utmost attention is given to the selection of material and the manufacturing of substantial trees, which for pattern and finish will compare favorably with any in the market."

Items listed for sale included "men's and ladies' riding saddles" and pack saddles. Hair cinches were offered "at $9 to $18 per dozen."[11]

There is no evidence that the saddlery business made much of a dent in the cost of keeping prisoners.

So how did the prison wind up in Salem?

For efficiency.

12. NOTES

1. Ronald B. Lansing. "The Tragedy of Charity Lamb, Oregon's First Convicted Murderess." *Oregon Historical Quarterly*, vol. 101, 2000.

2. Ibid.

3. The exact locations of their graves is uncertain, but Charity Lamb and other inmates are known to have been buried in Block 14—the southeast corner of Hawthorne's asylum cemetery. Today it is SE 20th and Morrison. Many Chinese immigrants also were buried in Block 14 because they were not allowed to be buried elsewhere. In about 1930 these graves—likely unmarked—were paved over, as Block 14 now belonged to Multnomah County. In 1952 county officials, thinking all the bodies had been removed years earlier, approved constructing an administration building on the site. In the early 2000s, after years of urging by activists, the county tore down the building and transferred Block 14 to the regional government, Metro. In 2019 voters approved a bond that will fund building a memorial on the site. See www.streetroots.org/news/2021/05/26/block-14-portland-s-lone-fir-cemetery-will-finally-get-its-due

4. Fred Lockley. "Reminiscences of Mrs. Frank Collins, nee Martha Elizabeth Gilliam." *Oregon Historical Quarterly*, vol. 15, 1916, pp. 358-72.

5. M'Naghten's Case, (1843) 10 Cl & F 200, 8 Eng Rep 718. Also, Old Bailey Proceedings Online February 1843. "Trial of DANIEL M'NAUGHTEN" https://www.oldbaileyonline.org/record/t18430227-874#

6. Bob Nikkel. Oregon Office of Mental Health Services, "A short history of the public mental health system of Oregon." 2000.

7. *Portland's Finest Past & Present*. Portland Police Bureau. Turner Publishing Co. 1999.

8. Chambreau first appears in this book in Chapter One as sole inmate of the Hudson's Bay Company's jail at Fort Vancouver.

9. Oregon Historical Society Archive document folders MSS 1535 and 550. Also, Finn John's website, "Offbeat Oregon," presents the story of Portland's temperance riots in an entertaining four-part series and lists scholarly sources.

10. Portland Police Museum and Historical Society and generally the writings of E. Kimbark MacColl, Portland city historian.

11. Oregon Historical Society Research Library, Imprint Collection No. 400 Box 9 Item 0680a. Portland OR.

13.
Administrative ease

When Oregon was admitted to the union in 1859, the governor and legislature decided to move all major institutions to Salem, the new state capital, to make them easier to supervise. Mainly that meant relocating the penitentiary from Portland.

The building obviously wasn't movable so the state was glad to unload it on Oregon Iron Works, a Portland foundry, for $6,000 although it had cost $85,000 to build.[1]

In October 1864, the Legislature appropriated $56,000, including what it got from the iron works, to "re-erect the penitentiary at Salem."

It was superintendent A.C.R. Shaw's task to move the approximately 60 prisoners to Salem in the spring of 1866.

According to a newspaper account published years later, they arrived "on Thursday, Friday or Saturday May 17th, 18th or 19th after a two-day trip by steamboat."[2]

The journey was less than 50 miles, so likely it was slowed by Willamette Falls. A steamboat obviously couldn't be portaged so that meant switching boats. Prisoners and guards would have had to do some walking and climbing. If all the prisoners couldn't be safely marched as one big group, a piecemeal transfer would have been necessary and would have taken time. And more than one boat may have been required because of the number of prisoners and guards.

With the whole prison operation moved to the new capital, officials had the opportunity to make a fresh start. They could decide from scratch what the new institution ought to look like and how it should be run. They certainly didn't want to replicate the leaky monument they'd erected in Portland, or the bumbling attempts to run it.

The Rev. George Henry Atkinson, one of Oregon's most distinguished citizens, was deputized by the 1865 Legislature to return East and see what other states were doing.

He came back with an exhaustive report covering everything from what kind of buildings they built to how they managed them. And he recommended reforms that went beyond the prisons, per se, and into the whole criminal justice system. He saw it as all of one piece.[3]

He thought uniform sentencing for criminal convictions was a good idea because not just because it was right but because it reduced tensions in prison. Convicts grew restive, he said, when they compared sentences, as they inevitably did, and one found he'd been sentenced to a much longer term for the same offense as another man for no other reason than that he drew a different judge.

Atkinson also had strong views on what kind of men should and should not be hired as guards.

He even discussed the benefits of good landscaping as a way to make prison more bearable and therefore more manageable.

The best prisons he visited, Atkinson said, were well-disciplined, efficient, secure, and humane, increasing the likelihood that inmates would leave the institution as better people than when they entered.

The surest way to get reform, he said, was to give inmates an education and vocational training and meaningful jobs to do while they served their time. He also believed in "good time"—allowing prisoners to shorten their sentences through good behavior.

Atkinson's impact on Oregon penology and education was all the more remarkable because he was an unelected and unpaid private citizen.

He was born into a prominent Massachusetts family that had made a fortune in shipping, insurance and real estate, but young George wasn't much interested in a business career.

After graduating from Dartmouth College, he attended Andover Seminary where he pursued religious studies and was ordained a Congregational minister. His Protestantism was of a progressive strain that believed in a better life in the here-and-now and not just the hereafter.

When Atkinson decided to migrate to Oregon, he and his wife took a merchant ship around Cape Horn, braving brutal seas and sharing quarters with a half-dozen other passengers and a food supply that included live pigs and chickens. Their luggage included boxes of schoolbooks for the free public schools they envisioned.

When the Atkinsons arrived in Portland harbor in the spring of 1848, they were relieved that the schoolbooks, still a scarce commodity in Oregon, had survived the voyage undamaged. It hadn't been a certainty due to the harsh conditions at sea that required them to hang hot cannonballs in wire cages near their berths to stay warm.

Atkinson's advocacy of free public schools won backing from Gov. Joe Lane whose first message to the Legislature recommended that every child in the Territory be educated without charge. Later on, Atkinson also would do more than anyone else to shape the character of Oregon State Penitentiary.

Prisoners arriving in Salem from Portland in 1866 were marched to a 26-acre meadow on the east edge of the new capital and put to work making bricks to build their own penitentiary.

The brickyard was inside a wooden fence and the temporary housing for the convicts was a wooden barracks that proved inadequate either as shelter or as a stopgap prison.

The fence was easy to climb, and 115 escapes were recorded in the first three months. That was more than the total number of prisoners, which meant that some escaped more than once. On Aug. 27, 1866, the entire convict population attempted a mass breakout.

It began when three inmates seized Supt. Shaw and Warden J.C. Gardner in the yard and forced them at knifepoint to march out the gate. Shaw yelled for the guards on the fence to open fire, but the guards were afraid they'd hit the officials.

Once through the gate, the hostage-takers abandoned their captives and ran for a woods on the edge of the prison property. The guards then began shooting and killed one, but the other two got away.

Amidst the confusion, all the other prisoners in the yard—about 50—rushed the gate and were met by officers wielding clubs and pick-handles. The fence guards also fired shots but, again, were afraid of hitting co-workers.

Eight convicts did manage to get away. There was no report of casualties from the gunfire.

For the next six years, Oregon State Penitentiary saw numerous efforts, some successful, to escape over the fence. Warden J. C. Gardner solved the problem by fitting prisoners with a new device he invented, the Gardner Shackle.

Also known as the Oregon Boot, it was a heavy steel ring fastened around one ankle. The ring weighed from five to 28 pounds and was supported by a steel stirrup that ran underneath the shoe. This kept the weight from resting directly on the ankle and causing injury.

Besides being hard to lug around, the heavy weight on one foot threw the prisoner off-balance and made running impossible.

When the Oregon Boot was introduced in 1866 it was welded on. Later models were removable.

Although the Boot did serve its purpose of reducing escapes, officials who succeeded Gardner condemned it as cruel and recommended it be outlawed.

"A great wrong we are compelled to put on the prisoners for want of sufficient walls is the (Gardner) shackle," Supt. W.H. Watkinds wrote to Governor Lafayette Grover in 1870, soon after taking the job.

> There are prisoners who have worn this implement of torture, known inside the prison as mankillers, until they are broken down in health and constitution. Young and strong men, with this steady weight, which pulls all day on their loins, yield after a few years, leaving the prison broken down physically, not from overwork or underfeeding, but simply from walking around to keep them from scaling the fences that are no protection without. Men lay in the hospital for weeks wearing these things suffering great pain and the begging to be relieved of the load. Your Excellency ordered a year ago that as few men as possible be ironed. This has been complied with but leaves many really and literally ironed down. Oregon state prison is the only place in the United States where this mode of murdering men by inches is practiced. It is murder and of the worst type.

Watkinds' view of the Oregon Boot was endorsed by the penitentiary's physician, Dr. A. H. Belt.

"A great tendency to disease of the kidney and weakness of the back with loss of muscular power in the lower limbs seems to be due to the wearing of what is called the Gardner shackle," Belt said in a letter that Watkinds forwarded to the governor. He continued:

> This is not a conclusion on a single instance but is the result of examination of every case that has been under my care. The rule has been that a few months only are necessary to destroy the health and consequent usefulness of everyone that has been subjected to their use, and in a few years at such a rate of deterioration, will destroy life. My impression is that while there may be speedier ways of ending life there are none that is surer. I would respectfully submit that if other means could be devised that would be equally safe, they be left off as soon as practicable.

Watkinds' successor, Supt. Benjamin Franklin Burch, wrote a similar message to Gov. Stephen Chadwick in 1878.

> Heretofore, it has been the practice to keep a large number of men heavily shackled to prevent escape, which renders them unfit for manual labor, injuring the constitution and holding them, as it were, by brute force…This principal I believe to be wrong. Such punishment can never lead to reformation and hence I am determined to dispense with it except as punishment, believing as has been demonstrated, they could be kept without it. By placing the shackles before them as punishment for violation of prison rules, I've been successful in keeping all but three, which three were trusties.

Burch said the shackle prevented men from getting completely into their bunks at night, exposing them to cold and preventing sleep and causing illness.

Gov. Chadwick took Burch's advice and abolished use of the Oregon Boot except under special circumstances such as preventing escapes during outside transport.[5]

During the wooden fence era, the State of Oregon bought brickmaking equipment to speed up construction of an updated penitentiary.

"The continued safe keeping of the convicts in a building no more secure than a common dwelling, and that is in a rapid process of decay, cannot be guaranteed," Gov. George L. Woods complained to the Legislature in 1870. The lawmakers had appropriated no construction money at all the prior year while funding the brick factory.

Tens of thousands of convict-made bricks were sold to commercial contractors who used them to build just about everything but a penitentiary.

Work on that project finally began August 24, 1871, marked by the laying of a cornerstone "with appropriate ceremony," as the Salem newspaper put it. Bricks from the prison brickyard at last were used for a prison.

13. NOTES

1. *Morning Oregonian*, Portland OR. Nov. 8, 1867, p. 3.

2. *Salem Statesman Journal*, Salem OR. Sept. 26, 1934, p. 4.

3. (See Appendix, p. 204.) Atkinson, "Report on Visit to Eastern Penitentiaries," *Journal of the Senate Proceedings of the Legislative Assembly of Oregon for the 4th Regular Session* (Salem, OR: W.A. McPherson, state printer, 1866), 504-20. Oregon State Library Special Collections. Atkinson's full report, submitted to penitentiary commissioners A.C.R. Shaw and J. H. Moores on Jan. 25, 1866, discussed the merits of the different eastern institutions he saw, but preferred the one in his home state of Massachusetts.

4. Watkinds was not known for tender feelings. In June 1871 he shot and wounded the editor of the Salem Weekly Statesman, S. A. Clarke, during an argument over politics.

5. Oregon boots were still offered for sale until fairly recently by several U.S. police equipment firms.

Afterword

As the frontier era came to an end in the 1870s, Oregonians likely couldn't have imagined what lay ahead for their hard-won penitentiary.

By September 2025, Oregon State Penitentiary would be just one of 10 state prisons with a combined inmate population of 8,744—more than the entire population of Portland in 1870. The prison archipelago would reach every corner of the state and employ more than 4,000 people including the administrative staff at the governing agency, the Oregon Department of Corrections.

All told, the annual budget would be nearly $3 billion, or approximately triple the amount the state would spend on its public universities.

Prisons were now big business and inevitably attracted the attention of Wall Street.

A private prison company, Corrections Corporation of America (CCA), now known as CoreCivic, was formed in 1983, and its first contract was to build and manage a detention facility for the Immigration and Naturalization Service. With so much money to be made, competitors entered the field, and some were listed on the New York Stock Exchange (NYSE), the two largest being CoreCivic (CXW) and The GEO Group (GEO)

Since private prisons would have a strong financial incentive to keep as many people in prison as long as possible, public policy groups warned that the trend could exacerbate a problem the United States already had—one of the highest incarceration rates in the world.

In June 2024, the U.S. Department of Justice reported that 2,048,524 individuals were imprisoned in 53 state and territorial prisons, with another 158,000, approximately, held in federal prisons. With 531 out of every 100,000 people kept behind bars, the U.S. rate of imprisonment was exceeded only by El Salvador at 1,086 per 100,000, Cuba at 794, Rwanda 637, and Turkmenistan 576. The rest of the world—just under half of all countries and territories—had rates below 150 per 100,000.

The cost of all this, not just in dollars but human lives, is incalculable, making it clear that prisons and prison policy deserve our attention, and more than sideshow treatment in the national debate.

Bibliography

19 George III. Ch 74.

21 George III. Chs. 68 and 71.

40 George III. Ch. 1. "An Act for the further introduction of the Criminal Law of England in this province, and for the more effectual Punishment of certain Offenders," enacted July 4, 1800. Published in *The Statutes of His Majesty's Province of Upper Canada*, 1818 edition.

40 George III. Ch 138.

40 George IV. Ch. 66, "An Act for regulating the Fur Trade and establishing a Criminal and Civil Jurisdiction within certain parts of North America," enacted by British parliament in 1821.

5 Elizabeth. Ch. 20, as adopted 1593.

9 George IV. Ch. 31, enacted June 27, 1828.

Abbott, Carl. *Portland in Three Centuries: The Place and the People.* Oregon State University Press, Corvallis OR. 2022.

Abbott, Carl. *Portland: Gateway to the Northwest.* Windsor Publications, Inc., Northridge CA. 1985.

Airey, William J. *A History of the Constitution and Government of Washington Territory.* PhD thesis, University of Washington. 1945.

Atkinson, G.H. "Report on Visit to Eastern Penitentiaries," *Journal of the Senate Proceedings of the Legislative Assembly of Oregon for the 4th Regular Session. 1866.* W.A. McPherson, state printer. Oregon State Library Special Collections. Salem OR.

Barnes, Harry Elmer and Teeters, Negley K. *New Horizons in Criminology.* Third ed. Prentice-Hall, Englewood Cliffs NJ. 1959.

Barry, J. Neilson. "Peter Corney's Voyages," 1814-17, *Oregon Historical Quarterly*, vol. 33. 1932.

Beaver, Herbert. Letter to Hudson's Bay Company governor and committee Oct. 10, 1837, HBC correspondence book HBC archives. Company records are kept at the Government of Canada archives: <https://central.bac-lac.gc.ca/.redirect?app=fonandcol&id=4193599&lang=eng>

Beaver, Herbert. Letter to the Aborigines Protection Society of London. Tract No. 8, 1842.

Beaver, Herbert. Letter to William Cameron McKay, May 27, 1840. William Cameron McKay Papers, MF 27. University of Oregon Library Special Collections. Eugene OR.

Blackstone, William. *Commentaries on the Laws of England*. Rees Welsh, Philadelphia. 1902.

Bonney, W. P. *History of Pierce County Washington*. Pioneer Historical Publishing Co., Chicago. 1927.

Bridges, Roger. *Journal of the Illinois State Historical Society*. Fall/Winter 2015.

Burnett, Peter H. "Recollections of an Old Pioneer," *Oregon Historical Quarterly*, vol. 5. 1904.

Carey, Charles H. *General History of Oregon*. Binsford & Mort, Portland OR. 1971.

Carey, Charles H., ed. "17th Anniversary Report, Methodist Annual Reports Relating to the Willamette Mission (1834-48)," *Oregon Historical Quarterly*, vol. 23. 1922.

Chambreau, Edouard "Frenchy." *Autobiographical Narrative for Years 1847-80*, Reed College Library collection. Portland OR.

Clark, Malcolm Jr. *Eden Seekers*. Houghton Mifflin, Boston. 1981.

Daniel Lee and Joseph H. Frost. *Ten Years In Oregon*. Arno Press, New York NY. 1973.

Davidson, J. N. *Negro Slavery in Wisconsin and the Underground Railroad*. Parkman Club Publications, 1897.

Dease, John Warren. *Memorandum Book, 1829*. MS, entry for Oct. 15, 1829.

Dennis, Elsie Frances. "Indian Slavery in Pacific Northwest," (three parts), *Oregon Historical Quarterly*, vol. 31. 1930.

Eisenburg, Nancy. *White Trash: The 400-Year Untold Story of Class in America.* Penguin Books. 2017.

Ermatinger, Francis. Letter to his brother, Edward, Feb. 26, 1839. Huntington Library, San Marino CA. HM 16761.

Glyndour Williams, ed., *Hudson's Bay Miscellaney*, Hudson's Bay Record Society, Winnipeg. 1975.

Goeres-Gardner, Diane L. *Necktie Parties.* Caxton Press, Caldwell ID. 2005.

Gray, William H. *A History of Oregon.* Harris & Holman, Portland OR. 1870.

Hager, Eli. *Debtors' Prisons Then and Now: FAQ.* The Marshall Project. 2015.

Harvey, Horace. "Some Notes on the Early Administration of Justice in Canada's North-West," *The Pioneer West.* Reprinted from *Alberta Historical Review.* Nov. 1953 and Jan. 1954.

Hines, Gustavus. *Oregon: Its History, Condition and Prospects.* Geo. H. Derby & Co., Buffalo NY. 1851.

Howard, John. *The State of Prisons in England and Wales.* Third ed., Warrington. Printed by William Eyres. London. 1784.

Hudson's Bay Company Correspondence Book, Fort Vancouver, 1838. Company records are kept at the Government of Canada archives: <https://central.bac-lac.gc.ca/.redirect?app=fonandcol&id=4193599&lang=eng>

Huff, Jim. *Portland Police to 1870.* Portland Police Museum and Historical Society. <www.portlandpolicemuseum.com/s/stories/portland-police-to-1870>

Hussey, John A. "Fort Vancouver Historic Structures Report," U.S. National Park Service. 1972.

Hussey, John A. "The History of Fort Vancouver and its Physical Structure," Washington State Historical Society. 1957."

Jackson County Administration, Series I. Jackson County, Oregon records, Box 067. University of Oregon Libraries, Special Collections and University Archives. Eugene OR.

Jessett, Thomas E., ed. *Reports and Letters of Herbert Beaver, 1836-38.* Champoeg Press, Portland OR. 1959.

Johansen, Dorothy O. *Empire of the Columbia*. Second ed. Harper & Row, New York NY. 1967.

John, Finn. *Wicked Portland: The Wild and Lusty Underworld of a Frontier Seaport Town*. The History Press. 2012.

Kelly, Joseph (Bunko). *Thirteen Years in the Oregon Penitentiary*. Portland OR. 1908.

King Charles II. "Charter incorporating the Hudson's Bay Company, 2nd May 1670," courtesy of Hudson's Bay House Library, Winnipeg.

Kingsnorth, Carolyn. "Pioneer Profiles: The Fathers of Jacksonville," *Jacksonville Review*. Jacksonville OR. February 2014.

Lansing, Ronald B. "The Tragedy of Charity Lamb, Oregon's First Convicted Murderess," *Oregon Historical Quarterly*, vol. 101. 2000.

Letter to the Editor, *The Oregon Daily Journal*. Sept. 27, 1953. Portland OR.

Lockley, Fred. "Reminiscences of Mrs. Frank Collins, nee Martha Elizabeth Gilliam," *Oregon Historical Quarterly*, vol. 17. 1916.

"Lone Fir Cemetery Will Finally Get Its Due," *Street Roots*. May 26, 2021. Portland OR.

M'Naghten's Case, (1843) 10 Cl & F 200, 8 Eng Rep 718.

Meany, Edmond S., ed. "Diary of Wilkes in the Northwest," *Washington Historical Quarterly*, vol. 16. 1925.

Minutes of the Council of Northern Department of Rupert's Land. Hudson's Bay Record Society. London. 1940.

Minutes of the Hudson's Bay Company 1679-82, 1st series. Hudson's Bay Record Society. London. 1945.

Morning Oregonian, Nov. 8, 1867. Portland OR.

Nikkel, Bob. "A short history of the public mental health system of Oregon," Oregon Office of Mental Health Services. 2000.

Old Bailey Proceedings Online February 1843. "Trial of DANIEL M'NAGHTEN" <www.oldbaileyonline.org/record/t18430227-874# >

Oregon Archives, "Journals, Governors' Messages and Public Papers of Oregon. Dec. 1, 1846." La Fayette Grover, ed. Asahel Bush, Public Printer, Salem OR. 1853.

Oregon Constitution, Article 1, Section 16.

Oregon Historical Society Research Library, document folders MSS 1535, 550. Portland OR.

Oregon Historical Society Research Library, Cayuse Five Trial Documents. File 1203. Portland OR.

Oregon Historical Society Research Library, Imprint Collection, No. 400 Box 9 Item 0680a. Portland OR.

Oregon Supreme Court Record. Stevens-Ness Law Publishing Co. Portland OR. 1938. pp. 7-8.

"Oregon Trail stories," <www.legendsofamerica.com/we-oregontrailaccount/>

Pethick, Derek. *James Douglas: Servant of Two Empires*. Mitchell Press Ltd., Vancouver, BC. 1969.

Pipes, Nellie B. "Indian Conditions in Oregon 1836-38," *Oregon Historical Quarterly*, vol. 32. 1931.

Pipes, Nellie B. ed., "Journal of John H. Frost," *Oregon Historical Quarterly*, vol. 35. 1934.

Portland City Archives, file AD/22569. Portland OR.

Portland's Finest Past & Present. Portland Police Bureau. Turner Publishing Co. 1999.

Pugh, Ralph B. *Imprisonment In Medieval England*. Cambridge University Press. 1968.

Radzinowicz, Leon. *History of English Criminal Law*. Stevens & Sons, London. 1848. I, 450-71.

Rich, E.E. ed., *History of the Hudson's Bay Company Vol II*. Hudson's Bay Record Society, London 1959, pp. 401-05.

Rich, E.E. ed., *The Letters of John McLoughlin: First Series, 1825-38*. The Champlain Society for the Hudson's Bay Record Society, London. 1941.

Rich, E.E. ed., *McLoughlin's Fort Vancouver Letters: Second Series, 1839-44.* Hudson's Bay Record Society, London. 1943.

Rich, E.E. ed., *The Letters of John McLoughlin, Third Series, 1844-46.* Hudson's Bay Record Society, London. 1944.

Rich, E.E. ed., *Simpson's Athabasca Journal.* Hudson's Bay Record Society, London. 1938.

Robertson v. Baldwin, 165 U.S. 275 (1897) Library of Congress.

Rothman, David J. *The Discovery of the Asylum.* Little, Brown, London. 1971.

Ruby, Robert E., & Drury, Clifford M. *The Cayuse Indians.* University of Oklahoma Press. 1972.

Sager, Catherine, Elizabeth and Matilda. *The Whitman Massacre of 1847.* Ye Galleon Press, Fairfield WA. 1997.

Salem Statesman Journal, Salem OR. September 26, 1934.

Scheflin, A., Van Dyke, J., "Jury Nullification: The Contours of a Controversy," *Law and Contemporary Problems*. National Criminal Justice Reference Service No. 73179 Volume 43, Issue 4. Autumn 1980.

Slacum, William A. "Slacum's Report on Oregon, 1836-37," *Oregon Historical Quarterly*, vol. 13. 1912.

Territorial document No. 13006, Oregon State Archives.

Territorial documents, 745, 445, 475, 524, 1035, 13006, Oregon State Archives.

The Cayuse Indians: Imperial Tribesmen of Old Oregon. Pacific Northwest National Parks and Forests Association. 1972.

Tobie, H.E. "Joseph L. Meek, a Conspicuous Personality," *Oregon Historical Quarterly*, vols. 39-41. 1938-40.

Townsend, John Kirk. *Narrative of a Journey.* Ye Galleon Press, Fairfield WA. 1970.

Transactions of the Annual Reunion of the Oregon Pioneer Association. Vol. 46. 1918. Annual publication of the Oregon Pioneer Association.

U.S. Statutes at Large 2 (1803):202. "An Act for continuing in force a law, entitled 'An act for establishing trading houses with the Indian tribes.' "
<www.govinfo.gov/app/collection/statute/>
United States Census Bureau, Federal Census (1850).

Vaughn, Thomas. "The Round Hand of George B. Roberts," *Oregon Historical Quarterly*, vol. 63. 1962.

Victor, Frances Fuller. "The First Oregon Cavalry," *Oregon Historical Quarterly*, vol. 3. 1902.

Victor, Frances Fuller. *The River of The West, Vol II*. Mountain Press Publishing, Missoula MT. 1985.

West, Oswald. "First White Settlers on French Prairie," *Oregon Historical Quarterly*, vol. 43. 1942.

Young, F. G. "Financial History of Oregon Part Two, Finances of the Territorial Period, 1849-1859," *Oregon Historical Quarterly*, vol. 8. 1907.

Young, F. G. "Finances of the Provisional Government," *Oregon Historical Quarterly*, vol. 7. 1906.

Appendix

(See ch. 13, p. 186.) The Rev. George Henry Atkinson wrote this extensive report about prisons he visited in 1865 in his "Report on Visit to Eastern Penitentiaries." It was printed in the Journal of the Senate Proceedings of the Legislative Assembly of Oregon for the 4th Regular Session, 1866.

Dear Sirs:

The structure of prisons and their discipline have of late years received much attention in England and in the United States. The great improvements made are comparatively of modern date, and Americans have been among the foremost to study the penal system and to perfect their penitentiaries. As an illustration, in the 25th report of the board of managers of the Massachusetts Prison Discipline Society, in 1850, they say: "The important points, which have been considered in the proposed extension of the state prison, of a general character, are convenience, classification, light, heat, ventilation, cleansing, solitary confinement at night, employment, instruction, humanity, discipline, order, (and) security against fire." These points were supposed to include all the interests of the public, and also of the prisoner. They indicate not only the results secured in the new structure at Charlestown, Mass., but also those which should be attained in all prisons old or new, and as such they may serve as an important guide in other inquiries and discussions. Noting them in their order, I first speak of the convenience of a prison. This pertains to location and internal arrangement.

[1.] Although the location of the Oregon penitentiary has been settled by vote of the people, it may be proper to remark that it compares in most respects favorably with the sites chosen in other states for these institutions. It has also the advantage of a stream of pure water for domestic and manufacturing purposes. It has a large area of land. Its vicinity to the capital, and to an intelligent, enterprising, moral and permanent population, and its nearness to a navigable river, favor both its discipline and economical management. It is to be hoped that it will prove healthful, and that no reason will exist for a change of site. The internal convenience of a prison depends upon a combination of advantages in its plan and structure, so that its operation can be conducted with system and thoroughness. The convict must be fed, clothed and kept cleanly. But it was not convenient to do this, if the effort had been made, in the English prisons, where Howard found fifty or a hundred, or even two hundred prisoners in a single room, and where Mrs.

Fry found three hundred women in two rooms. There they saw their friends, and kept their multitudes of children, and they had no other place for cooking, washing, eating and sleeping. It is not the most convenient to care for a dozen prisoners of all classes locked up in a single room, in which they sit, eat, converse and sleep. The time for such arrangements has passed. The modern penitentiary furnishes a cell for every convict. The room, though small, is sufficient for all his wants while in it. Two systems still prevail in taking meals — the old congregate system, in which all sit and eat together at tables with guards over them. This is the custom in the New York, Ohio, and other western prisons. The other method, in which every convict takes his food to his own cell and eats it alone, prevails at Charlestown. While the convicts have their hour for meals, with doors barred, the guards and officers have the same hour, off duty, for their meals uninterrupted, and thus no time is lost in the establishment.

To accomplish this, the kitchen, cell-rooms and guard-rooms must be conveniently and compactly arranged. To secure this, the prison at Charlestown begins with a central octagonal rotunda four stories high. The kitchen is in the basement, and being central, the food is passed through windows to the prisoners as they go from their shops to their rooms. From three sides of this octagon, wings extend for cell-rooms. From the fourth side the wing for the officers' quarters is built. Over the kitchen is the guard-room, open through gratings on all sides. The four other narrower sides are used for long grated windows. Standing at this center a single guard can see all the prison areas, the yards, shops, and officers' rooms, by simply turning round, and can go to any part through a grated door and down an iron staircase. The chapel is over the guard-room, and the hospital is designed to be above the chapel, away from the noise of machinery, both having iron stair-cases from the corridors along the cells of all the wings. This compact structure permits the officer to have the oversight of the entire prison, day and night, without exposure. It gives to every prisoner the same light and air as the officer enjoys.

The other prisons visited, had usually a central building divided into several rooms, each commanding a view of only a part of the cells or areas from a single point, and that through a grated door or a concealed aperture. In them the culinary and heating departments are usually kept separate. At Charlestown the cooking and heating apparatus are in the central kitchen, from which pipes, conveying steam or hot water, radiate to all the wings. The cell-rows are in the center of the wing, three, four and five stories high, double with broad, cool areas around, extending to the walls, high as the ceiling. In the walls are high, broad windows, similar to those in the penitentiary at Portland, affording an abundance of light and air. The cell-rooms of the New York, New Hampshire, Ohio, Illinois and other prisons visited, were similar, though not united to a central rotunda. The, old idea of cells along the walls, and slots in the walls to each cell to give light and air has for the most part been given up.

[2.] Security is the next point to be noticed. This was, originally, the chief idea of a prison. It seems always to have been a problem with governments what to do with criminals. How to keep them securely. In the earliest times they seem to have been thrust into slimy dungeons. Under Roman law, free citizens, if convicted, were reduced to slavery and committed to the care of a master, or compelled to labor on public works. The English early resorted to transportation of convicts to America and Australia. At one time, their prisoners were confined in old hulks in the Thames. At another, they were huddled into close rooms, debtors, thieves, murderers, young and old; healthy and diseased, in one mass, to pollute and be polluted. But the chief reliance has been upon strong walls of stone and iron; suggested, probably, by the old feudal castles, which were used for such purposes. Security is sought in most of the prison visited, but having a system of cells of stone or brick, with iron doors, which are entirely enclosed in a stone or brick building. The prison yards are enclosed by thick walls of stone or brick, from twenty to twenty-five feet high. In addition, armed guards are constantly stationed in towers on the walls. As much reliance, perhaps, is placed upon the vigilance and courage of the guards as upon the buildings.

[3.] The supervision of prisoners when in their cells is gained on the rotunda plan more thoroughly than on any other. The turnkey or sub-warden can see any movement or hear any sound from any cell without moving from his place, or he can pass in his felt slippers to any part of the area or corridors unobserved, His central position enables him to give instant alarm to officers in the rear or to watchmen on the walls.

[4.] It has been felt of late years, that prisoners ought to be classified. This was one of the reforms proposed by John Howard in England and on the continent. The wardens and official visitors of prisons, assent to its importance. It is an evil to put a man guilty of larceny in companionship with a murderer, or a youth with an old and hardened offender. But the contract system seeks for workmen and makes no distinction among them. All classes mingle together in the shop. The evil can be in part obviated by having a watchman in every shop, as at Charlestown, Auburn and Columbus, who allows no conversation between the prisoners.

[5.] Solitary confinement at night is deemed exceedingly important for the convicts as well as for all objects of justice. "If a man," says Mr. Buxton, "has the misfortune to be committed for examination to a London prison, guilty or innocent, he is locked up -with perhaps a half dozen of the worst thieves, or at night he may find himself in bed and in bodily contact between a robber and a murderer, or between a man with a foul disease on one side and one with an infectious disorder on the other." What was true there, has been true in every prison. The only remedy is a cell for every man, and to have every man in his room alone. This method assists the discipline, prevents corrupt communications and the concocting plans to escape.

[6.] Employment of prisoners of all classes is essential to discipline and good order. In the earlier English and Scotch prisons convicts had nothing to do. Vulgar, profane and vicious conduct were the result. Then the treadmill was introduced, with no object but to compel work. Latterly, prisoners have been at once set upon some useful employment. The aim in Massachusetts is to give everyone a trade, if he had not one before, so that he can earn his living, and also to discipline him to habits of labor, that he will earn it. The same general idea prevails in all our penitentiaries. To accomplish it large and airy work-shops are erected, various kinds of machinery are introduced, with good motive power, and the whole conducted by the state, or the shops are rented to contractors for periods of five or ten years, who furnish the machinery, and a definite number of men are furnished for a contractor's work, at prices varying from forty cents to one dollar per day. The wardens retained perfect control of the government of all the shops. All our late prisons have improved workshops, in many cases they are two stories high. The convicts seem as earnest and skillful in their work as if they were free laborers. It gives them health, cheerfulness and relieves the tediousness of their confinement.

[7.] Instruction has of late been found an important aid in prison discipline. At Charlestown no regular teacher is provided or regular times set apart for lessons, except the chapel and Sabbath services. At Auburn and Columbus, teachers are paid to instruct the convicts after their daily tasks are done. Many who know not how to read or write have there learned. Libraries are furnished for prisoners, and also writing materials, and lights are furnished till nine o'clock, p. m., so that they can improve themselves. The chaplain is usually the librarian. All letters to or from the convicts are first submitted to the warden or the chaplain for inspection. These means softened the hardened offender and operate to restore the wanderer. Especial reliance is now placed upon religious services. At Charlestown the convicts have a choir among themselves and a melodeon. The choir spend a half hour every day in practicing tunes for the next morning service. It has been found that a very small per cent of discharged criminals are returned for a second term. In those prisons which give the least attention to ordinary or religious instruction there is more natural distrust and more insubordination, and more temptation to cruelty. Officers find the benefit of these means. We are to remember that prisoners are men, and that many of them have been untaught. A chapel and schoolroom are an important part of the structure.

[8.] Humanity is made a distinct consideration in the structure and discipline of modern prisons. The tendency of prisons is to promote inhumanity. It requires great self-control on the part of keepers to guard the convicts, and yet refrain from tyranny, and at the same time give them due care. Prisoners are considered, and they are usually, bad men — frequently the worst characters in community. Entering their cells under the force and restraints of law, they instantly feel themselves cut off, outcasts from society, banished, abandoned and degraded. They naturally seek to form a society of their own, hostile to that outside their prison. They as naturally cherish revenge, and having no way to reach the public, they often vent their feelings upon their keepers. They soon show their corrupt and vicious characters. They expose themselves, by their violence, passion, deception and baseness, to receive the same in return.

Some jailors at last consider it unwise to show them any kindness or special attention. They confess that their own feelings of humanity are changed toward prisoners by contact with them, and they distrust all attempts to reform them, or to benefit them. The public always share, to some extent, in these feelings, especially those who attend much upon our courts and who become familiar with criminal life. Both the prison and the prisoner are avoided, the one as hopeless of good and the other of improvement. But to carry out the humane ideas of Howard and other philanthropists, it is essential not only that the hospital be suitable in every respect for the comfort and restoration of the sick, but that the physicians, the wardens, the guards, the watchmen and the overseers, be humane, moral, self-controlled, as well as firm and courageous men. The Massachusetts and Ohio state prisons are good examples of the humane system as carried out in American prisons. It is often remarked that frequent changes of officers are injurious in this and in other respects to the management of prisons. It has also been suggested that the appointing power be in the hands of the supreme court of the state, and that occasional visits of the judges to the prison might be highly useful.

[9.] Light is made a point of special importance in the structure of modern prisons. Light is found to be as necessary to health as food and exercise, and nowhere more than to persons confined in buildings. Nearly all the late prisons have long windows in both sides. The aim is to give the prisoner as much as the keeper enjoys. There are eight windows, each 22x8 feet in the external walls of the Charlestown prison, making the area around the cells almost as light as the open court. The cells have an open grated door of 6x2 feet dimensions. The sun shines in by day and the gas or oil lamps from the area at night. The prisons of other states have almost equal facilities for light. At San Quentin, California, the buildings consist of a system of cells opening to the yard, without an enclosing prison. But the doors being of iron plate, admits of less light than the grated doors in proper cell-rooms. Besides, prisoners can have no light at night.

[10.] Heat is a more important consideration to prisoners than to those who have their freedom. It must be abundantly and steadily supplied or they will suffer. It is hardly less needed in our damp climate than in the extremely cold ones. The method of heating at Charlestown is by means of pipes of steam or hot water extending round the area. In some other places stoves are still used. Furnaces are proposed in some cases.

[11.] Ventilation is applied not only to the areas by means of long windows, and by apertures and gratings in the ceiling, but to every cell by a tube running to the top of the building, or into flues which extend to the top.

[12.] Water and cleansing are deemed very important to the comfort and safety of our prisons. By means of pipes and faucets an abundant supply is furnished in all the wings, and convenient to every prisoner at Charlestown, and everyone is required to wash himself daily, and to bathe once a week. The opportunity and means for personal cleanliness are furnished in other prisons visited, but not to the same extent and thoroughness. An abundant supply of pure cool water is found to be essential to the cleanliness of the establishment and to the health of the inmates of such institutions, if possible, more than in any other. Many prisoners are naturally uncleanly, while the restraint upon liberty perhaps destroys any self-respect and habit of cleanliness more quickly than any other condition. Were they neglected, and allowed to do as they please, doubtless their condition in these respects would become intolerable. Such was the case in English and continental prisons before the times of reform.

[13.] Discipline, though entering into every feature of a prison, deserves a separate notice. The structure favors or hinders it. All penitentiaries should be designed to impress the prisoner with the idea that he is securely confined, and that any attempt to escape will be useless. This is the first element in his proper control. Broken walls, defective cells and careless guards set convicts on the watch to escape and defeat all discipline. He has lived uncontrolled. He has broken law, defied authority, despised government, trampled upon the rights of men, and claimed impunity in the reckless gratification of his own appetites and passions. For his own good and the public welfare life must feel like absolute and complete restraint of his liberty. For this the massive walls and iron gratings must take the place of the majesty of law which he has defied. Rejecting the one, he must feel the other.

A second means is the constant supervision of an officer day and night. This, in several of our best conducted penitentiaries, is to prevent all conversation between convicts.

A third element of his discipline is keeping regular hours for sleep, for work, for meals, and for the recreation or reading or writing or study, and for religious worship.

A fourth means is the single cell for everyone. Convicts rooming together destroy discipline. Cliques are formed in prison which plot evil and involve newcomers, and cause much disturbance.

A fifth means is punishment for refractory conduct. In some prisons, as at Michigan City, Ind., and San Quentin, Cal., the whip is used. In the latter, also chains and the dungeon. In some prisons the shower bath and the iron collar are used. In others the solitary dark cell with barely bread and water enough to support life, are the penalties for the rebellious. But the prisoner is allowed at Charlestown to come out at the moment he is willing to go to work and do his duty, and seldom does one stay in the "solitary" twenty-four hours.

A sixth means of discipline is work, regular and steady, of some profitable and instructive kind. This is usually in shops, and the prison laborers seem like others in similar trades elsewhere. Work is now relied upon more than anything else to control and, if possible, to reform convicts.

A seventh means is the system of commutation for good behavior. In some prisons two days in a month are allowed, but these are increased to five days for long terms, so that a man sentenced for ten years may, by good conduct, get free in about eight years. But if he rebels, all his gains are liable to be lost. He is put upon his self-control. He forms a habit of it and of labor, and thus often is fitted to become a better citizen than ever before.

An eighth means of discipline is careful, attentive, experienced, humane, thoroughly temperate, well-trained keepers; not brutish, passionate, violent, profane and cruel men. More depends upon officers and guards than upon the prison itself.

A ninth means of discipline is some provision for discharged prisoners by which they can enter upon civil life again with hope of support and respectability. In Massachusetts, besides teaching the convict a trade, an agent is appointed by the state to see every convict before his discharge, inquire what he wishes to do, and then either send him to his home newly clad in citizen clothing free of charge, or to find a place for him to work at his trade, the employer only knowing his history, or to board him a week or two at a good place until he can find employment.

Other states give discharged prisoners a few dollars and send them away without care. But the kindness shown him at this moment, when peculiarly exposed, is opportune, and it saves some a second fall. The hope of it imparts confidence to the mind of the convict that he has friends left, and it stimulates him to prove himself worthy of their regard.

[14.] The orderly arrangement of a prison ought to be simple, compact, complete and convenient for all the purposes of security, health, work, comfort and discipline. No prison has these points combined more fully than that at Charlestown, though all have them to some extent.

[15.] For security against fire, the floors, walls, doors, galleries, stair cases, fastenings, grates, are iron, stone or brick, and there is nothing combustible in the structure except the window frames and the ceilings over the areas of the prison at Charlestown, so that, although not absolutely fire-proof, it is nearly so. The new prisons of the western states are made of stone, iron and brick and are nearly fire-proof.

[16.] Extension is an important item in a prison in a new state. If it can be it ought to be done in harmony with an original plan, and without changing the mode of supervision. The central rotunda permits such extension by a wing on each of the four sides whenever wanted. The second wing will be as convenient and easily guarded as the first. On other plans the wings could be placed out of reach. The new buildings at San Quentin stand side by side away from the guard room. The plan of the prison ought to be a unit in itself, so complete and suggestive that all future additions will naturally grow out of it, as branches grow from a stock, and so that there will be no good reason to depart from it.

[17.] The comfort of the prison officers is an important element in the construction and provisions for a prison. It is coming to be understood that these officers ought to be gentlemen in the true sense of the term, intelligent, dignified, courteous, free from narrow prejudices, firm and kind, for they are to be entrusted with absolute power over men, and over men whom they will have some strong provocations to misuse and to injure. And if it becomes the state to choose such men as superintendents, wardens, sub-wardens, clerks, physicians, chaplains, teachers, guards and watchmen—men who will respect each other—it becomes the state to furnish them with good, comfortable, neat, and tasteful quarters in the prison structure. They are sequestered from society; they endure a kind of imprisonment. At least one or more of them will have his family within. The head officer needs a room suitable to receive visitors. For this purpose one wing of the rotunda can project without the walls, and be equally convenient and safe. Besides good quarters, these officials merit, if faithful, liberal salaries. They have great responsibilities. They are confined day and night to the same positions. They are subjected to insults and exposed to dangers from the vicious and reckless, who would murder them in an instant for the sake of escaping, and yet the utmost vigilance, prudence, and courage are expected of them. The state which exacts so much of its servants for the public good, ought to reward them with a fair compensation, such as their standing and similar duties would elsewhere command.

[18.] The expenditure for a prison will be considered by every citizen. In order to a fair estimate of this subject, it is important to keep in mind the cost of crime before the prison is reached by the criminal. Consider the damage he has done to person and property — to the public peace and prosperity. Consider, also, the cost of courts, of officers, and of trials. Consider, furthermore, the need of depriving him of his liberty, and the danger of his escape; and, above all, consider the means and the duty, if possible, of his reform. A single crime often costs not only life but thousands of dollars to community, and unless we subject the criminal to the most sure and wise imprisonment, we encourage crime and multiply losses and evils to an indefinite extent. In this view, if a suitable prison be expensive, still it ought to be built, not extravagantly, but thoroughly. The cost of the octagonal building and one wing, at Charlestown, Mass., with fixtures, was one hundred thousand dollars, fifteen years ago. The new prison at Joliet, Ill., had cost, a year ago, over seven hundred thousand dollars, and estimates were then made for expending one hundred and seventy-nine thousand dollars more upon it; and, possibly, when completed it will cost one million dollars. The new prison at Michigan City, Ind., will cost, as per estimate, from four to five hundred thousand dollars. Indiana will then have two prisons. The state prison of California has cost, I was in formed, several hundred thousand dollars. The cost of the older prisons cannot now be ascertained. Much can be saved by the employment of the prisoners in making brick and in the construction of some portions of the edifice and walls.

[19.] Convict labor is a subject which will continually be discussed by officers of prisons and a portion of the outside public. The question is asked, whether the state should employ the convicts in its own workshops, and make the profits, or whether it will furnish shops and sell their labor at a given rate per day to contractors? The former method is the most troublesome; the latter is perhaps less remunerative. In the former, however, the state classifies and controls the convicts better for their discipline and welfare. In the latter case, contractors are apt to get an undue influence in the prison management. The former may be the best investment, but the latter yields the surest income. The contract system prevails in nearly all the prisons visited. It works -well, if the prison officers are permanent, and are sustained in the complete control of the shops and yards, so as to preserve the prison discipline; and provided, also, that the demands for workmen shall be kept subordinate to the objects of the prison itself. Contractors often use strong and skillful workmen, and crush the weak. It is money against discipline at one moment, and against humanity at another. On the other hand, the labor of convicts, being very cheap, enables either the state or the contractor to compete with free labor, so as to drive the latter out of market. The saddlery and collars, and brick, perhaps, made at San Quentin, California, are beginning to control the San Francisco market, and to drive other men from the business. The same tendency appears with their boots and shoes and flannel shirts. The furniture, brushes, whips, barrels, and castings, made at Charlestown, Mass., have the same tendency in Boston, and it is only overruled by the great extent of the market. The prison contractor enjoys a kind of monopoly, which largely compensates for all his risks. In a few cases, prisons have become self-supporting by their convict labor. In other cases, the annual deficiency varies from $10,000 to $50,000. The monthly income of the San Quentin prison is $2,400, and the monthly expenditure about $7,000.

[20.] All expenses of the Charlestown prison, in 1860: $80,243
-All receipts, mostly for labor: $80,747
-Being an excess of receipts: $504
-In 1855, ordinary disbursements were: $52,611
-Ordinary receipts: $40,915
-Deficit: $11,695
-The income of the New Hampshire state prison at Concord, for 1863: $12,417.
-Expenses for the same year: $8,451
-Gain to the state: $3,965
-In 1865, expenses exceeded receipts: $471

[21.] Prison statistics are now made to include all important facts concerning prisoners. For example, the Massachusetts tables give us the whole number received and the whole number discharged; ages of convicts; crimes, periods of sentence; states and countries of which they are natives; places of conviction; previous employments; expiration of sentences; life sentences; and the crimes; re-commitments; number of convicts per year and per month; and their daily rations of food. To keep such accounts and compile these statistics accurately in the larger prisons requires all the time of a clerk. The information is of more value than its cost.

[22.] Prison clothing. This subject is awakening some discussion. The black and white striped cloth is still worn in nearly all prisons. Its value is to prevent escape, and to expose for easy detection a man who has escaped. An effort is made in Massachusetts and California to furnish prison clothing with less distinctive marks.

[23.] Apartments for females are usually within the same enclosure of walls, but in a separate building, and under the care of a matron. That at Columbus, Ohio, seems to be very well conducted, and to be a model for such a department.

[24.] Adornment of the grounds is now a noticeable feature of some of our best prisons. The yard is laid off with neat walks, grass plats, flower beds, and occasionally a fountain of water and a few trees. It is desirable, for both officials and prisoners, to have both shade trees and flowers in these grounds.

[25.] Insane prisoners form a peculiar class, for whom strong rooms have to be specially provided. In some cases they are sent to asylums, and re-committed after recovery, but the guardians of the insane generally object to receiving them.

[26.] The subject of unjust or inconsistent imprisonment is receiving the attention of gentlemen familiar with the details of prison life. It is found by the officials in their acquaintance with prisoners that men guilty of the same crimes are committed for very different periods — as one man for five years for stealing and another for fifteen years for exactly the same offence. When prisoners become aware of the facts, and they always do so, they feel the injustice and become more reckless. Others are found guilty of no crime, but merely unfortunate dupes of their associates. Such cases call for a careful discrimination in the discipline, and a more frequent inspection by the officers of the law.

[27.] The architecture of a prison with all its departments for security, labor, comfort and improvement, is a subject demanding careful study and a close observation of the practical workings of prison discipline. Incomplete and unsuitable structures spring from imperfect plans and ideas. Among the foremost in the knowledge of this subject, so far as I was able to ascertain, were the architects of the new prison buildings at Charlestown, Mass., and of the new jail at Boston.

Respectfully submitted,
G. H. Atkinson,
Visitor for Commissioners of Oregon penitentiary

Acknowledgments

I owe all of these people more than I can say, and I've probably forgotten others who also deserve to be on this list, and for that I'm sorry.

Tom Vaughan, longtime executive director of the Oregon Historical Society; Hoyt C. Cupp, a warden of Oregon State Penitentiary; J.C. Keeney, a deputy warden and warden of Oregon State Penitentiary; Harol Whitley, a deputy warden of Oregon State Penitentiary; George E. Sullivan, a superintendent of Oregon State Correctional Institution; Gordon Little, former inmate Oregon State Penitentiary; Dorothy O. Johansen, author and professor of history at Reed College; Arden X. Pangborn, an editor of the Oregon Journal; Ed O'Meara, a city editor of the Oregon Journal; J. S. Murray, a chief clerk of Oregon State Penitentiary and former guard at Yuma Territorial Prison; Thomas E. Gaddis, author of *Birdman of Alcatraz* and co-author of *Killer: A Journal of Murder*; Dr. Dean Brooks, an administrator of Oregon State Hospital.

To friends and family, Dee Lane, James Long, Jr., Steve Long, Jenny Niemeyer, Ruby Long, Therese Bottomly and Susie Marchese.

Also, a huge thank-you to the library and archives staff at the Oregon Historical Society in Portland, and the staff of Oregon State Library and Archives.